Hera I'm the queen of the gods and goddesses, *not* the Queen of Mean.

Hera Zeus may be the mightiest god on Olympus, but he's going to be in the doghouse when he gets home.

 Zeus
Now, honey, you know I love only you.

 Aphrodite
Hello? Did somebody say Love?

 Echo
LOVE! LOVE! LOVE! LOVE! LOVE! LOVE!
LOVE! LOVE! LOVE! LOVE! LOVE! LOVE! ...

 Athena
Pipe down, Echo. I'm planning a surprise.

 Medusa
You wanna see a surprise? I'll show you a surprise!

Daphne Hey, can somebody please scratch my back, er, bark?

 Cerberus
BARK!

 Echo
BARK! BARK! BARK! BARK! BARK!
BARK! BARK! BARK! BARK! BARK! ...

 Eros
Hey, everybody, watch what happens when I shoot this lead arrow. *Zing*!

 Zeus
Hi, honey, I'm home!

 Furies
Uh-oh ...

CONTENT CONSULTANT
William Hansen
Professor Emeritus of Classical Studies and Folklore
Indiana University, Bloomington

Library of Congress Cataloging-in-Publication Data

Bryant, Megan E.
She's all that! ; a look-it-up guide to the goddesses of mythology /
Megan E. Bryant.
p. cm. -- (Mythlopedia)
Includes bibliographical references and index.
ISBN-13: 978-1-60631-027-4 (rlb.)   978-1-60631-059-5 (pbk.)
ISBN-10: 1-60631-027-5 (rlb.)   1-60631-059-3 (pbk.)
1. Goddesses--Dictionaries, Juvenile. I. Title.
BL473.5.B79 2009
398'.4509495--dc22

2009017168

MYTHLOPEDIA

SHE'S ALL THAT!

I love you all!

A Look-It-Up Guide to the Goddesses of Mythology

MEGAN E. BRYANT

SCHOLASTIC

SHE'S ALL THAT!

PROFILES and MYTHS
Up close and personal with the gods of the pantheon

I thought we were BFFs!

Callisto

I can't *bear* to look at you!

Artemis

THE MYTHLOPEDIA INTRODUCTION

Are you ready to get your myth on? Then you've come to the right place: MYTHLOPEDIA, your one-stop shop for everything you need to know about the stars of Greek mythology. From gods and monsters to goddesses and heroes, the myths that rocked the ancient world are ready to rock yours—if you're ready to read on! But first, check out a little background info that will help you make sense of these amazing characters and stories.

So, what is mythology?

Good Question! "Mythology" is the word used to describe *all* the myths of a particular society. People who specialize in studying myths are called "mythologists." From the Yoruba of West Africa to the Inca of South America, from the Norse of Europe to the Navajo of North America, every culture has its own myths that help us understand its customs and ways of viewing the world.

What is a myth?

Simply put, a myth is a kind of story. But not just any old story! Most myths have one or more of these characteristics:

- Myths are usually about gods, goddesses, or supernatural beings with greater powers and abilities than ordinary humans.

- Myths explain the origins of the world or how human customs came to be.

- Myths take place in a time long, long ago, usually in the earliest days of humanity (or just before humans showed up on Earth).

- Myths were usually thought to be true by their original tellers—no matter how wild or strange they seem to us.

TWO NAMES, POWERS THE SAME

Many gods and goddesses have both Greek and Roman names. That's because the ancient Romans adopted a great deal of Greek mythology and made it their own, often by changing the name of a particular god or goddess. Generally, that deity's powers and myths stayed the same— even though he or she had a new name. As a result, the study of Greek and Roman mythology is often grouped together under the name "classical mythology."

> ## What is the purpose of myths?

A better question might be, What *isn't* the purpose of myths? Myths can:

➤ explain how things came to be—like the origin of the universe or the creation of humans;

➤ teach people about the values and beliefs that are important in their society; and

➤ contain deep religious significance to the people who tell and believe in them.

Perhaps most importantly, studying myths can teach us about people around the world—their cultures and what is (or was) important to them.

> ## Do myths really matter today? After all, mortals have reality TV.

Absolutely! References to Greek mythology are all around us.

➤ Ever heard of Nike brand athletic gear? Meet Nike, personification and goddess of victory.

➤ What would Valentine's Day be without the god of love, Cupid—or Eros, as the ancient Greeks called him?

➤ Does *Apollo 13* ring a bell? The first crewed U.S. space missions were named for Apollo, the god of archery and prophecy.

Bottom line: References to ancient myths are everywhere, from science to pop culture, and knowing about them will help you understand more about the world we live in.

HOW DID WE LEARN THESE STORIES?

At first, Greek mythology was passed along orally through storytelling, songs, and poetry. We learned the stories from written versions, mainly Homer's epic poems *The Iliad* and *The Odyssey*, which tell about the great deeds of heroes. Other sources are Hesiod's *Theogony*, which describes the origins of the world and the gods, and the *Homeric Hymns*, a collection of poems addressed to different gods.

SAT

SHE'S ALL THAT

What was a typical day like for a goddess on Mount Olympus? In a word: busy! One powerful goddess was the actual Earth; she gave birth to the sea, the sky, and some hideous monsters. Another goddess was responsible for agriculture—especially grains (her Roman name gave us the word for cereal), and one cheerful goddess managed to get the sun up every morning. A group of goddesses presided over childbirth and determined the length of each new life; another group inspired the great artists and thinkers.

Although they were revered by humans for hundreds of years, the goddesses weren't perfect. One goddess was known for her jealous, manipulative, and vengeful ways (no, no, not *you*, Hera!). Another goddess bribed a judge in a beauty contest, setting off a chain of events that started a war. Still, the Greeks built temples to them and honored them with sacrifices and rituals.

Later, many of the Greek goddesses were adopted by the Romans as their own and given Roman names, such as Venus (Aphrodite), Minerva (Athena), and Diana (Artemis). We could go on and on, but the goddesses can say it so much better themselves. So get ready, mortals. You're about to get up close and personal with some of the boldest, cleverest, and most powerful goddesses of Greek mythology!

Hera Here's the goddesses' honest truth ...

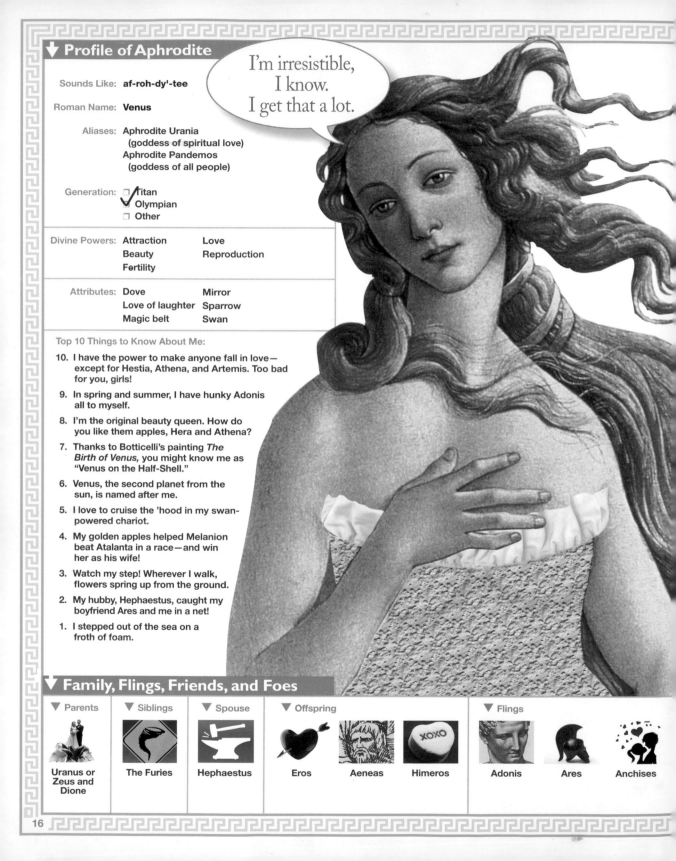

▼ Profile of Aphrodite

I'm irresistible, I know. I get that a lot.

Sounds Like: **af-roh-dy'-tee**

Roman Name: **Venus**

Aliases: Aphrodite Urania
(goddess of spiritual love)
Aphrodite Pandemos
(goddess of all people)

Generation: ☐ Titan
☑ Olympian
☐ Other

Divine Powers: Attraction   Love
Beauty   Reproduction
Fertility

Attributes: Dove   Mirror
Love of laughter   Sparrow
Magic belt   Swan

Top 10 Things to Know About Me:

10. I have the power to make anyone fall in love—except for Hestia, Athena, and Artemis. Too bad for you, girls!

9. In spring and summer, I have hunky Adonis all to myself.

8. I'm the original beauty queen. How do you like them apples, Hera and Athena?

7. Thanks to Botticelli's painting *The Birth of Venus,* you might know me as "Venus on the Half-Shell."

6. Venus, the second planet from the sun, is named after me.

5. I love to cruise the 'hood in my swan-powered chariot.

4. My golden apples helped Melanion beat Atalanta in a race—and win her as his wife!

3. Watch my step! Wherever I walk, flowers spring up from the ground.

2. My hubby, Hephaestus, caught my boyfriend Ares and me in a net!

1. I stepped out of the sea on a froth of foam.

▼ Family, Flings, Friends, and Foes

▼ Parents	▼ Siblings	▼ Spouse	▼ Offspring			▼ Flings		
Uranus or Zeus and Dione	The Furies	Hephaestus	Eros	Aeneas	Himeros	Adonis	Ares	Anchises

APHRODITE

ALL U NEED IS ♥

Since I stepped out of the sea foam, it's been Hel-*lo* Romance! The gods on Olympus are 2GTBT! Except for Zeus—who ordered me to marry that loser Hephaestus! Heph fell so hard for me that he wove me a magical golden belt that makes me *more* irresistible than I was before (LOL). Now Ares and Adonis totally ♥ me. BTW, I also won a beauty contest that just *might* have started a war.

XOXOXO

> You look lovely, but could you please try on another outfit?

Hephaestus

▼ Friends

Helen of Troy

Paris

Melanion

The Graces

▼ Foes

Helios

Hera

Artemis

Hestia

Athena

APHRODITE

"I am simply irresistible."

MYTHLOPEDIA

IT'S GREEK TO ME

The Birth of Venus was painted by Italian artist Sandro Botticelli around 1483. It shows the love goddess Aphrodite (her Roman name is Venus) rising out of the sea on a shell. This painting explains why Aphrodite is sometimes called "Venus on the Half-Shell."

"Spread the love!"

SEA FOAM SWEETHEART

The goddess of love steps out of the sea in a froth of foam.

A goddess as gorgeous as Aphrodite was too special to be born in an ordinary way. After the Titan Cronus mutilated his father, Uranus (the sky), he threw some of Uranus's body parts into the sea. The waters began to foam and froth. Suddenly, from the foam rose the beautiful goddess of love, Aphrodite. The waves carried her to the island of Cyprus, and as Aphrodite stepped onto land, flowers sprang up beneath her feet. Now that's what you call making an entrance!

REALITY CHECK

The Greek word for foam, *aphros*, sounds similar to Aphrodite's name. How appropriate, since the goddess was born in a froth of sea foam!

Zephyrus

Aphrodite

FAIREST OF THEM ALL

Aphrodite wins a beauty contest—and starts a war!
All the gods and goddesses were gathered at a wedding, except for one: Eris, the goddess of discord. Annoyed that she hadn't been invited, Eris started trouble by tossing a golden apple marked "For the Most Beautiful" into the reception. The goddesses Aphrodite, Hera, and Athena each claimed that the apple was intended for her, and they began to argue. The mighty god Zeus decided that Paris, prince of Troy, should settle the argument by judging a beauty contest. Each goddess contestant offered Paris a bribe, hoping that he would choose her as the most beautiful.
Paris couldn't resist Aphrodite's offer: She promised to make him irresistible to Helen, the most beautiful woman in the world. Helen was already married to Menelaus, king of Sparta, but that didn't stop Paris. The prince kidnapped Helen and took her to Troy. The Greek hero Agamemnon led an expedition to rescue Helen, igniting the Trojan War.

> "Well, *obviously* the apple was meant for me. I mean, *duh!*"

Aphrodite

Himeros   Eros

Up top!

High five, Bro!

BIG BABIES

Sons of the love goddess share the love.
The goddess of love was always accompanied by her sons Eros and Himeros. Eros (Roman, Cupid) is the better known of the two: He was the god of love. With his gold-tipped arrows he could arouse love in anyone he chose to shoot—god or **mortal**. But Eros also had lead-tipped arrows that could inspire loathing. Himeros was the god of longing. He, too, had a bow and arrows that he used on gods and mortals. Unlike Eros, Himeros was a minor god who was paid little attention by mortals except for those he shot.

REALITY CHECK

When Shakespeare's Romeo first sees Juliet, he says, "Did my heart love till now? Forswear it, sight!/ For I ne'er saw true beauty till this night." Perhaps he was struck by one of Eros's arrows!

Want to know more? Go to:
http://shakespeare.mit.edu/romeo_juliet/full.html

FIRST ANNUAL MOUNT OLYMPUS BEAUTY CONTEST!
Official Entry Form

Name: *Aphrodite*   Eyes: *Ocean blue*   Hair: *Heavenly gold*   Special talent: *Love, and lots of it!*

What is your greatest asset?
Wow, this question is so hard to answer! My beautiful blue eyes? My long, lustrous hair? My perfect skin? As amazing as those are, my greatest asset is probably my ability to spread love. And who doesn't love LOVE?

Who is your hero?
Well, probably myself, because I make everyone so happy when they are in love, and also I am so beautiful.

Final Notes: *I'm so excited to be a contestant for the title! I just know you're going to love me!*

LOVES AND MARRIAGE
A homely husband works for his wife's affection.

The moment Aphrodite arrived on Mount Olympus, her power to inspire desire caused all the gods to fall in love with her. Zeus feared that the gods would fight one another for her hand in marriage, so he ordered Aphrodite to marry Hephaestus, the god of fire and patron of craftsmen. Zeus chose Hephaestus because he was known to be dependable. He was also the only ugly Olympian.

Like the other gods, Hephaestus fell in love with Aphrodite. Unfortunately, the goddess of love didn't love him back, so Hephaestus used his skills as a craftsman to try to win her affection. He wove a beautiful golden belt for her that made her even more attractive and irresistible to others. Bad move!

Hephaestus

The original happy family ... NOT!

Aphrodite

Eros

HEPHAESTUS NETS A PAIR OF LOVEBIRDS
The sun god tattles and Hephaestus sets a trap.

Aphrodite wasn't about to let a little detail like marriage interfere with her love life. Soon after her wedding to Hephaestus, the goddess fell madly in love with Ares, the god of war. One day, when Hephaestus was away, the sun god Helios spied Aphrodite and Ares together. When Helios told Hephaestus about his wife's cheating ways, the godly blacksmith set a trap for the lovers. He crafted an invisible net and draped it around his wife's bedchamber. The next time Aphrodite and Ares were together, SNAP! Trapped! Hephaestus invited all the Olympians to view the sneaky lovebirds, but instead of being outraged, they thought it was hilarious.

Adonis wasn't a ba-a-a-d guy.

MESSING AROUND WITH MORTALS
Aphrodite falls for not one but two adorable shepherds.

The love-crazed goddess was soon gaga over Adonis, a beautiful young shepherd. Aphrodite had given baby Adonis to Persephone, queen of the **Underworld**, for safekeeping. But with one look at the adorable boy, Persephone fell in love with him, too, and refused to give him back.

One day, while hunting on Earth, Adonis was killed by a wild boar (probably sent by the jealous Ares). Aphrodite pleaded with Zeus to return Adonis to her. But Zeus, not wanting to anger Persephone, decided that both goddesses should share the boy for eternity: Adonis would spend spring and summer with Aphrodite on Earth and the rest of the year with Persephone in the Underworld.

Later, Aphrodite had an affair with another **mortal**, the shepherd Anchises, with whom she had a son, Aeneas. He was her last mortal boyfriend.

"I love wrath almost as much as I love … love!"

LOVE HURTS
The jealous goddess of love psychs out the competition.

Aphrodite was well known for her wrath against people who displeased or disrespected her. Psyche, a beautiful mortal woman, suffered because of Aphrodite's jealousy. Fearing that Psyche was getting more attention than she was, Aphrodite ordered her son Eros to use his arrows to make Psyche fall in love with an ugly man. Instead, the moment Eros saw Psyche he fell deeply in love with her.

In the meantime, an **oracle** had told Psyche's father to leave his daughter on a cliff, where a suitable husband would find her. Lifting her from the cliff, the wind god Zephyrus carried Psyche to

P.U.! What stinks?

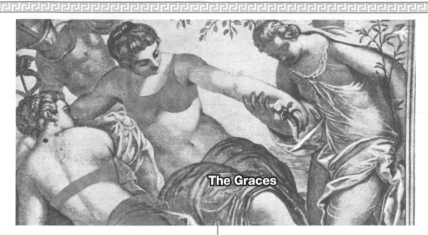
The Graces

a palace, where Eros joined her during the night and left before dawn, warning Psyche to never look at him. Psyche's jealous sisters suggested that Eros (now her husband) might be a monster. So that night the goddess snuck a peek at him. When Eros awoke and saw Psyche looking at him, he flew away.

Psyche begged Aphrodite to help her win her husband back. Instead, the goddess of love assigned a series of nearly impossible tasks for Psyche to complete. Finally, Zeus made Psyche **immortal** so that she and Eros could be together and Aphrodite was appeased.

In another story, Aphrodite was furious that the women of Lemnos had stopped worshipping her. So she **afflicted** them with such terrible body odor that their husbands all left them for new wives!

APHRODITE'S ATTENDANTS
Guess who's the most popular goddess in the group?

Aphrodite was so beautiful and beloved that she almost always attracted a crowd. In addition to her boyfriend of the moment (Adonis or Ares) and her sons (Eros, Himeros, and Aeneas), Aphrodite had many female friends. The Graces, female **personifications** of charm, joy, and beauty, were naturally drawn to Aphrodite, as were the Hours, who represented the harmony of the natural order. Among her other friends were Chloris, a goddess of flowers, and her husband, Zephyrus, the god of the warm west wind and spring. Both enjoyed Aphrodite's company.

Life can be a bear!

Sounds Like: ahr'-tuh-mis

Roman Name: Diana

Aliases: Cynthia, Potnia Theron, Locheia, Agrotera, Kourotrophus

Generation: ☐ Titan ☑ Olympian ☐ Other

Divine Powers: Chaste love
Childbirth
Hunting
Women
Youth

Attributes: Bear Hound
Bow Moon
Deer Silver arrow
Delos Temple at Ephesus

Top 10 Things to Know About Me:

10. The day after I was born, I helped my mom deliver my twin brother, Apollo.

9. When I was young, I begged my dad, Zeus, to let me stay a maiden forever.

8. I demand that the nymphs who follow me maintain their purity—and if they don't, I punish them! Right, Callisto?

7. As goddess of the hunt, I lead my BFFs through the woods, seeking wild game.

6. If a man threatens my virtue (or that of my followers), I'll hunt him down!

5. Aphrodite and I don't see eye-to-eye on love.

4. Orion was my friend—until he got *too* friendly, so I killed him.

3. I protect the young of all creatures. Itty-bitty, fwuffy-wuffy bunnies are so cute!

2. Like my brother Apollo, I can heal people—or make them sick.

1. My silver arrows can bring women a peaceful, painless, and permanent sleep!

▼ Family, Flings, Friends, and Foes

▼ **Parents**

Zeus and Leto

▼ **Siblings**

Apollo **Athena**

▼ **Friends**

Selene **Hippolytus** **Nymphs** **Chiron**

ARTEMIS
TOUGH STUFF

Get a grip, girls. Those boyfriends you're always boo-hooing about aren't worth the trouble. Take it from me—I'm bad to the bone and never waste a moment wondering if some guy is into me or not. Not convinced? Join me for a hunting party tonight, and you'll see my point. Meet me by moonlight, and don't forget your bows and arrows—I'd lend you mine, but you don't want to touch the silver ones!

REALITY CHECK

The Artemis 30 is an antiaircraft weapon used by the Greek armed forces. It is effective against both ground targets and low-flying targets.

Want to know more? Go to: http://www.haf.gr/en/mission/weapons/artemis.asp

This is going to hurt!

Artemis turned her friend Callisto into a bear and shot her!

▼ Foes

| Aphrodite | Orion | Hera | Callisto | Actaeon | Niobe | Agamemnon |

ARTEMIS

"Girlz rule!"

MYTHLOPEDIA

Ἄρτεμις

IT'S GREEK TO ME

How were the Greek gods and goddesses worshipped? Many had temples dedicated to them, where public religious rituals were held to honor them. These rituals often included animal sacrifices, athletic contests, and dramatic performances. Other rituals were private, conducted by individuals.

Some **deities**, like the goddess of grain, Demeter, and the god of wine, Dionysus, were the focus of mystery cults—top-secret groups that promised participants a better existence, both during life and after death.

Temple of Hephaestus

A BUMPY BIRTH

Artemis's mother wanders the world to find a shady spot.

Artemis and her twin brother, Apollo, were the children of Leto and the great god Zeus. Zeus's wife, Hera, was well known for her jealous rages, which were usually directed at her husband's romantic partners and his children with them. When Hera learned that Leto was pregnant with Zeus's twins, she came up with a particularly awful punishment: She forbade Leto to give birth anywhere on land, or anywhere that the sun shone. Poseidon, the god of the sea and Zeus's brother, took pity on Leto. He revealed a small part of Delos, an island that had previously been underwater. There, Leto gave birth to Artemis, who then helped deliver her own brother, Apollo, cementing her role as a goddess of childbirth.

REALITY CHECK

Delos is an island considered sacred by the ancient Greeks, who built temples and statues there to honor the gods. It is in the Aegean Sea, near the island of Mykonos.

I helped my brother OUT!

Artemis

Apollo

Callisto

This is sooooo unfair!

SILVER SLEEP

Artemis's silver arrows promise a gentle death to women.

Like her brother Apollo, Artemis had healing powers. She also had the power to sicken or even kill women. She would shoot her silver arrows to deliver a painless death to women. It was often said that a woman who died during childbirth had taken an arrow from Artemis.

PURITY POWER

A goddess gets the okay from her dad to stay single— forever.

When Artemis was a little girl, among the favors she asked of her father, Zeus, was that she be allowed to remain a **chaste** maiden forever. Zeus granted her request, promising his daughter she'd never have to marry. Artemis demanded that her followers remain chaste, too. If one of her followers left to get married, Artemis would bless the union. But if Artemis caught one of her followers with a boyfriend, she would fly into a terrible rage. Callisto, a favorite companion of Artemis, learned this the hard way when she gave birth to Zeus's son Arcas. An outraged Artemis turned Callisto into a bear and shot her!

REALITY CHECK

According to myth, after Artemis killed Callisto, Zeus placed Callisto in the sky as the constellation Ursa Major, which takes its name from *ursus*, the Latin word for "bear." Her son Arcas became Ursa Minor.

Want to know more? Go to:
http://www.windows.ucar.edu/tour/link=/the_universe/Constellations/circumpolar/ursa_major.html

Ursa Major

Artemis

> "I'm not that kind of goddess."

"This will hurt me more than it hurts you!"

ARTEMIS AND ORION
A beautiful friendship ends in a painful way.

No goddess or **mortal** woman was a better hunter than Artemis—so it was logical that she and Orion, himself a great hunter, would be close friends. But their friendship took a terrible turn when Orion, attracted to Artemis's beauty, tried to strike up a romance with the goddess. Artemis was so disgusted by Orion's advances that she killed him for daring to get a little too friendly. According to other stories, Gaea created a scorpion that attacked and killed Orion after he boasted about his hunting skills.

REALITY CHECK
According to myth, after the great hunter Orion was killed, Zeus placed him in the sky as the constellation Orion; beside Orion, Zeus placed a scorpion (Scorpio).

Constellation of Scorpio

ATTACK ON ACTAEON
Artemis turns the hunter into the hunted.

Actaeon was a great hunter who had the misfortune of offending Artemis and paying a dear price. One day, while he was hunting in the woods, Actaeon wandered away from his hunting party. He came to a hidden pool where Artemis and her attendants were bathing. Actaeon made the mistake of watching them for just a moment—and they caught him looking. Furious, Artemis turned Actaeon into a stag. Actaeon the stag was then attacked and killed by his very own dogs.

REALITY CHECK
The painting *Diana and Actaeon* (1556–1559) by Titian, an Italian Renaissance master, depicts Actaeon encountering Diana (the Roman name for Artemis) and her attendants while they bathe.

Want to know more? Go to:
http://www.nationalgallery.org.uk/

"What's this world coming to when a goddess can't take a bath in peace?"

Actaeon

Artemis

Formerly Actaeon

Artemis

Apollo

Niobe

Niobe's children

AGAMEMNON'S CHOICE
The wind goes out of Agamemnon's sails.

When the Greeks declared war on the city of Troy, they chose Agamemnon as their leader. As the Greeks sailed toward Troy, their fleet was held up at Aulis by **adverse** winds sent by the goddess Artemis because Agamemnon had offended her. To appease Artemis and secure a favorable change of wind, Agamemnon agreed to sacrifice his eldest daughter, Iphigenia, to the goddess. At the last moment Artemis spared the girl's life and allowed the wind to fill the Greek ships' sails.

THE PRICE OF PRIDE
Niobe brags about her kids and loses every one of them.

Niobe was a mortal woman who had fourteen children—seven handsome sons and seven beautiful daughters. One day, she made a fateful mistake. She boasted that she was a better mother than the goddess Leto, Apollo and Artemis's mom, because she had seven times as many children.

Artemis and Apollo weren't about to let anyone criticize their mother, especially not some ordinary mortal. With her silver arrows and accurate aim, Artemis shot and killed every one of Niobe's daughters. Apollo used his arrows to shoot and kill all of Niobe's sons. Niobe, realizing that her bragging had caused the deaths of her children, was consumed by grief. She sobbed constantly, until Zeus turned her to stone. Even then, the stone continued to weep.

> "My aim is even sharper than my silver arrows!"

Artemis

Eros

▼ Profile of Athena

Sounds Like: uh-thee'-nuh

Roman Name: Minerva

Aliases: Pallas Athena
Parthenos
("the maiden")

Generation:
☐ Titan
☑ Olympian
☐ Other

Divine Powers: Handicrafts
Industry
War
Wisdom

Attributes:
Aegis	Olive tree
Armor	Owl
Golden staff	Serpent
Helmet	Shield with Medusa's
Lance	head on it

I have a great idea!

Top 10 Things to Know About Me:

10. My dad, Zeus, has over 140 kids—but I'm his favorite!

9. Talk about making an entrance—I popped out of my dad's head all dressed up and ready to go!

8. I'm a real brainiac!

7. I leave the bloodshed to my brother Ares. I'm more interested in the strategic side of warfare.

6. I sided with the Greeks during the Trojan War.

5. Building the Trojan Horse was my idea. I love a surprise!

4. I turned Arachne into a spider for bragging that she was a better weaver than me. After all, I am the goddess of handicrafts!

3. I became the patron of Athens by creating the first olive tree. Sorry, Poseidon, you lose!

2. The Parthenon is my greatest temple—and it still stands today! (It's named after one of my nicknames, Parthenos.)

1. Nike, the goddess of victory, is my BFF. That girl plays to win!

▼ Family, Flings, Friends, and Foes

▼ Parents

Zeus and Metis

▼ Siblings

Apollo

Artemis

Ares

▼ Friends

Nike

Odysseus

The Greeks

Asclepius

Heracles

ATHENA

SMARTY-PANTS

Know everything? Me? You're too kind! It's true that I created the olive tree and perfected the arts of weaving, cooking, and pottery—all things that made life better for humans. And I've never lost a battle, because I put a lot of thought into my strategy (you can give a little credit to my pal Nike). Well, yes, that Trojan Horse I dreamed up was *awfully* clever, wasn't it? What can I say—I'm just gifted!

REALITY CHECK

On the Acropolis in Greece, you can still visit a temple dedicated to the goddess Athena.

Want to know more? Go to: http://www.ancient-greece. org/architecture/athena- nike.html

Good thinking, Athena!

▼ Foes

Arachne   Poseidon   Ares   The Trojans   Hephaestus

Athena gave the people of Athens an olive tree, so they named their city for her.

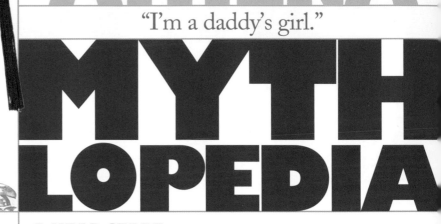

ATHENA

"I'm a daddy's girl."

MYTH LOPEDIA

IT'S GREEK TO ME

A **prophet** is a channel, or speaker, of divine, or godly, truth. The word *prophet* comes from the Greek meaning "one who speaks for another." Because prophets' messages frequently contain predictions of the future, they also **foretell**. In Greece, prophets were connected to certain shrines, like Apollo's temple at Delphi. Their main responsibility was interpreting the secret messages of the **oracle**. These messages came in different forms, such as dreams or moving leaves.

Oracle at Delphi

A HEAD START

Athena is born with a bang— right out of her daddy's head! Before the mighty god Zeus married Hera, he was married to Metis, who was known for her unmatched wisdom. But then Zeus learned of a worrisome **prophecy**. It was predicted that one day Metis would bear a son greater than Zeus himself. With news like that, Metis and Zeus's marriage began to go bad— especially since Metis was

already expecting their first child. To solve the problem, the mighty Zeus swallowed Metis whole, preventing her from bearing any children. Lucky for Zeus, clever Metis continued to advise him from within, making him especially wise.

Years later, Zeus was stricken with a splitting headache. In agony, he allowed the handy god Hephaestus to whack him in the head with an ax. This cured more than Zeus's headache. It delivered his daughter Athena, who sprang from her father's head fully formed and dressed for battle! She soon became Zeus's favorite child, and the only one he trusted with his powerful tools—his **aegis** and his thunderbolts.

Hephaestus

OUCH!

Zeus

WARRING SIBLINGS

Fighting begins at home for these warring siblings.

Mount Olympus was home to two war **deities**, half siblings Ares and Athena. Why did the ancient Greeks need two deities of war? Because Ares and Athena played very different roles. Athena focused her energy on **strategy**. She was also interested in the skills of warfare. She wasn't bloodthirsty, but instead saw war as a necessary evil. When a war was fought, Athena supported the side that was morally right, and she intervened to make sure that justice was served.

Ares represented the savagery of war. He was passionate about violence and slaughter and didn't care which side was right or wrong. As a result, Athena was generally more liked and respected than Ares—by both gods and **mortals**. During the Trojan War, Athena and Ares found themselves backing opposite sides: Athena supported the Greeks, while Ares supported the Trojans. During one battle, Athena jumped into the fight to help a soldier attack Ares. Ares then raced home to Mount Olympus so that Zeus could heal his wounds.

Back off, Ares!

Athena

Ares

> "Ugh, Ares is so violent! What's his problem?"

Victory shoe

SPOTLIGHT ON NIKE

Athena and Nike, BFFs.

Nike was more than just the goddess of victory, she was also the **personification** of the concept of victory itself. The winged goddess Nike, with her laurel and palm branches, presided over all battles and athletic events.

Nike

Before any sort of athletic contest or battle, ancient Greeks would pray to Nike for her favor. Like the other gods and goddesses, Nike had great respect for Athena. There is a temple dedicated to Nike on the Acropolis in Athens, next to the Parthenon.

REALITY CHECK

The famed athletic gear company Nike, which takes its name from the goddess of victory, was founded by Bill Bowerman, a track-and-field coach at the University of Oregon, and Phil Knight, a runner from Portland. The Nike swoosh was created by a design student at Portland State University.

Want to know more? Go to: www.nike.com

A CRAFTY SURPRISE

Arachne weaves herself a tangled web.

Athena was the patron of handicrafts such as pottery and weaving—skills that greatly benefited humans. In one myth, a girl named Arachne foolishly bragged that she was a better weaver than Athena. So Athena disguised herself as an old woman and tried to warn Arachne about the consequences of such boasting.

> "Don't blame me—I gave the girl a chance to show a little respect!"

But Arachne claimed she would gladly challenge Athena to a weaving contest and, if she lost, accept any punishment. The old woman revealed herself as Athena, and she and Arachne began to weave. At the end of the contest, Athena had to admit that Arachne's woven tapestry was perfect. Nevertheless, the humiliated Athena tore Arachne's work to shreds, broke her loom, and hit her on the head to teach her a lesson about upstaging a goddess. Overcome with guilt, Arachne tried to hang herself, but Athena showed mercy. She **transformed** Arachne into a spider and turned the noose around her neck into a spiderweb. Ever since, Arachne and her children have populated the world as spiders.

Athena

Arachne

REALITY CHECK

Arachne is the Greek word for "spider," and is the root of the English word *arachnophobia*, which means "fear of spiders."

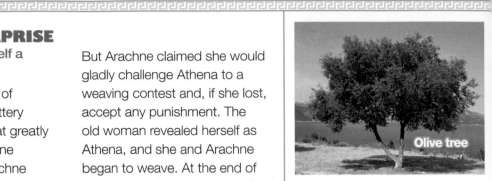
Olive tree

ATHENA'S ATHENS

The greatest city in Greece is named for Athena.

Athena and her uncle Poseidon, the god of the sea, wanted the same thing: **patronage** of a great Greek city. So they held a contest to decide who would get it. Each created a gift for the people of the city. Poseidon struck the ground with his **trident** and a great fountain of water shot up. The people were amazed! But the water was salty and of no use for growing crops or drinking. Apart from its beauty, the fountain was a worthless gift. Then Athena revealed her creation: an olive tree. The simple olive tree was a tremendous gift. It provided food, oil for cooking and light, and wood for building and heating. Athena was immediately named the patron, and the city took its name, Athens, in a show of gratitude to the clever goddess.

THE GIFTED GODDESS

A whisper from Athena causes inspiration to strike even mere mortals.

Athena used her intelligence to inspire some of the greatest creations of the ancient world. During the long and brutal Trojan War, Athena supported the Greeks. She gave the Greek hero Odysseus the idea that would eventually win the war: the Trojan Horse.

To the ordinary person, the Trojan Horse looked like a giant wooden statue of a horse. But inside, it had a secret compartment that was large enough to hold several soldiers. The soldiers hid in total silence, keeping perfectly still, while the Greeks left the horse outside the gates of Troy as a parting gift from Athena herself. Then the rest of the Greek soldiers pretended to sail home.

The Trojans brought the horse inside the gates, believing it to be nothing more than a gift that celebrated their triumph in the war. Late at night, while the Trojans slept, the Greek soldiers crept out of the horse and opened the gates to the city. The entire Greek army poured into Troy. They killed many men, captured many women and children, and took control of the city. As a result of this battle, the Greeks destroyed Troy and won the war.

REALITY CHECK
Was there really a Trojan Horse? No one knows for sure but there are many reconstructions, like this one in Turkey.

Odysseus

Athena

Surprise!

Sounds Like: daff'-nee

Roman Name: Daphne

Aliases: Laurel

Generation:
- ☐ Titan
- ☑ Olympian
- ☑ Other

Divine Powers: A freshwater nature spirit

Attributes: Laurel tree
Water

Top 10 Things to Know About Me:

10. My father, Peneus, is a river god.

9. I'm a Naiad—a freshwater nymph. Nereids, Dryads, Oceanids, and Oreads are some other types of nymphs.

8. I pledged to stay pure forever— no boyfriends!

7. Leucippus loved me so much he dressed up as a girl to spend time with me!

6. My friends and I were really upset about Leucippus's lie, so we killed him.

5. I *was* a happy-go-lucky nymph.

4. Eros shot Apollo with one of his gold-tipped arrows so he'd fall in love with me.

3. Eros shot me with a lead-tipped arrow so that I wouldn't love Apollo in return.

2. Apollo is such a pest! He wouldn't take no for an answer.

1. When I called my daddy for help, he found me a great hiding place— permanently.

▼ Family, Flings, Friends, and Foes

▼ Parents

Peneus and Creusa

▼ Siblings

Hypseus **Cyrene**

▼ Flings

Apollo

DAPHNE

LEAF ME ALONE

Dad, when I shouted "Save me from Apollo!" did you hear "Turn me into some dumb tree that has no fun"? Because that's what you did! I loved being a pretty nymph. Now look at me! I'm totally covered with bark. If I'd wanted to put down roots, I would have married Apollo. And my hair, well, it looks like a bird's nest! Oh, wait, that *is* a bird's nest. Just leaf me alone—you wouldn't understand!

REALITY CHECK

Most laurels are evergreen trees and shrubs. They grow best in warm climates and are characterized by the aroma of their bark and their leathery, simple leaves. The true laurel, or sweet bay, is native to Anatolia, in Turkey. You might know these as bay leaves, which are used in cooking.

Want to know more? Go to: http://oregonstate.edu/dept/ldplants/lano2.htm

To protect her from Apollo, Daphne's dad turned her into a laurel tree.

▼ **Friends**

Nomia

Aegle

Lilaea

▼ **Foes**

Leucippus

Apollo

Eros

DAPHNE
AND THE NYMPHS
MYTHLOPEDIA

Δαφνη

IT'S GREEK TO ME

Nymphs were female spirits associated with natural elements, such as rivers, streams, oceans, meadows, and trees. They protected certain features of the landscape and beautified the natural world. They were known for their youthful beauty. Although they were not **immortal**, nymphs lived for hundreds of years.

There were many different categories of nymphs, including:

- ➤ **Dryads**—woodland nymphs
- ➤ **Oreads**—mountain nymphs
- ➤ **Limoniads**—meadow nymphs
- ➤ **Napaea**—valley nymphs
- ➤ **Naiads**—freshwater nymphs
- ➤ **Nereids**—sea nymphs
- ➤ **Oceanids**—land and water nymphs
- ➤ **Limniads**—lake nymphs

HIDE-AND-SEEK

A prank goes wrong—and Daphne pays the price. Daphne, a Naiad, pledged herself to **chastity**. One day Apollo, the god of archery, teased the god of love, Eros. Apollo joked that Eros's arrows were not as powerful as his own. He even joked that Eros should give up his bow and arrow forever, and use just his torch to influence love.

Eros didn't like that one bit, so he decided to show Apollo just how powerful he could be. Eros shot the handsome god with a gold-tipped arrow to make him fall in love with the nymph Daphne; then he shot Daphne with a lead-tipped arrow to make her hate Apollo.

Apollo, who had never been in love before, went crazy with love for Daphne and chased her through the woods. Filled with loathing for the god, Daphne ran to the banks of the river. Just as Apollo reached out to grab her, the terrified nymph cried to her father, the river god Peneus, to save her. In an instant Daphne was **transformed** into a laurel tree! Heartbroken, Apollo declared that the laurel tree would be sacred to him; he is often depicted with a laurel wreath on his head.

"I'd get you for this, Eros, if I weren't rooted to the ground!"

METIS WORKS IT FROM THE INSIDE

Zeus swallows his wife and ends up with a splitting headache.

Wise Metis, an Oceanid, was Zeus's first wife. A **prophecy** revealed that one day Metis would give birth to a son more powerful than Zeus. This prediction filled Zeus with worry—especially since Metis was expecting their first child. To prevent the prophecy from coming true, Zeus swallowed Metis whole!

Many years later, Zeus had a terrible headache. Desperate for a cure, he begged the god Hephaestus for help. Hephaestus obliged by hitting Zeus on the head with an ax. From the gash in Zeus's head sprang his full-grown daughter Athena. The precocious goddess had inherited her mother's wisdom. (In fact, some stories say that the great Zeus himself wasn't all that wise until he swallowed brilliant Metis.)

SYRINX'S SORROW

Syrinx hides in the reeds and ends up making music.

Pan, the wild half-man, half-goat god of nature, had a soft spot for nymphs—but the feeling wasn't mutual. Pan had a crush on the Naiad Syrinx. But Syrinx, a follower of the goddess of the hunt, Artemis, had pledged herself to chastity and wanted nothing to do with the fun-loving god.

Pan wasn't about to give up. He chased the terrified Syrinx while she begged her sister nymphs to save her. And save her they did! Syrinx was instantly transformed into the hollow reeds that lined the river's edge.

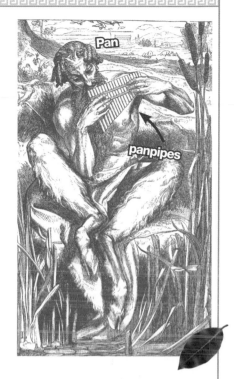

Pan

panpipes

Frustrated, Pan broke some of the reeds and discovered that the wind blowing across them made a haunting musical sound. He tied together different lengths of reed, and the syrinx, or panpipe, was created.

REALITY CHECK

The syrinx, or panpipe, is a wind instrument identified with the nymph Syrinx and the god Pan.

nymph

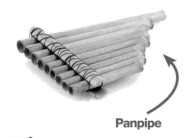

Panpipe

Sounds Like: dih-mee'-tur

Roman Name: Ceres

Aliases: Doso, Deo

Generation:
- ☐ Titan
- ☑ Olympian
- ☐ Other

Divine Powers: Agriculture and crops (especially grains)
Bringer of the seasons
Fertility

Attributes:

Basket	Pig
Bundle of wheat	Snake
Crown of wheat	Torch
Fruit	Vegetables
Grain	

> Don't *make* me come down there!

Top 10 Things to Know About Me:

10. My dad, Cronus, swallowed me whole after I was born!

9. I gave the gift of grain to humans.

8. When my daughter Persephone was kidnapped by Hades, I was too upset to do my job, so humans starved.

7. I disguised myself as a mortal and searched high and low—maybe not low enough—for Persephone.

6. I cursed Erysichthon for cutting down a grove that was sacred to me.

5. The Eleusinian Mysteries were secret ceremonies held in my honor.

4. I showed Triptolemus how to sow grain so that he could teach other humans.

3. My family is a little bit complicated. Just ask my brothers!

2. Most grains, fruits, and vegetables are under my control. You can thank me next time you put berries in your cereal!

1. I tried to make Demophon a god—until his mom interfered.

▼ Family, Flings, Friends, and Foes

▼ Parents	▼ Siblings					▼ Offspring	▼ Flings	
Cronus and Rhea	Zeus	Hades	Poseidon	Hera	Hestia	Persephone	Poseidon	Zeus

DEMETER

HAVE YOU SEEN HER?

MISSING: My daughter

NAME: Persephone

DESCRIPTION: Beautiful goddess

MISSING FROM: Earth

CIRCUMSTANCES: Was picking flowers with mom and friends. Reportedly got into a dark-colored chariot, license plate: dead2U. Driver described as creepy. Last seen entering gates of the Underworld.

COMMENT: Persephone, come home. Am pouring your favorite cereal.

CONTACT: If you have any information regarding the whereabouts of this girl, please contact demeter@grain-goddess.mt-o

MOM! Hades is bothering me!

Persephone

▼ Friends

Arion

Ploutos

Philomelos

King Celeus

Triptolemus

Demophon

▼ Foes

Hades

Metanira

Erysichthon

DEMETER

"Who's hungry?"

MYTHLOPEDIA

Δημητηρ

IT'S GREEK TO ME

There are two generations of Olympian gods and goddesses. The first generation includes the offspring of Titans, siblings Zeus, Demeter, Hades, Hera, Hestia, and Poseidon. The second generation includes Zeus's offspring Aphrodite, Apollo, Ares, Artemis, Dionysus, Hermes, and Hephaestus.

Olympians

GOT GRAIN?

The goddess of grains gives a great gift to humans.

Demeter, the goddess of grains, was one of the most worshipped **deities** in ancient Greece. Her gift of crops led people to settle in towns and cities, and abandon their difficult lives as **nomadic** hunters and gatherers. The primary grains grown in ancient Greece included barley, wheat, and millet. All these grains could be used to make breads or porridge cereals. According to ancient stories, Demeter taught Triptolemus, a son of King Celeus, how to **sow**, or plant, grain. Then she gave him a dragon-powered **chariot** so that Triptolemus could travel the world and teach the skill to all humanity.

REALITY CHECK

Demeter's Roman name, Ceres, is the origin of the English word *cereal*, which is usually made of grain.

"Enjoy the breakfast of champions— it's on me!"

Demeter's work!

MOTHER LOVE

Demeter yearns for her daughter and makes humans long for food.

Demeter had several children, but Persephone, her daughter with Zeus, was her pride and joy. She loved Persephone with her whole heart and took her everywhere; this mother-daughter pair was practically inseparable. But one day, Demeter let Persephone out of her sight—and disaster struck.

Demeter had no idea that Hades, ruler of the **Underworld**, had made a secret arrangement with Zeus for Persephone's hand in marriage. One afternoon Persephone was picking flowers with some of her **nymph** friends, Hades roared up in his chariot and kidnapped the girl, dragging her back to the Underworld with him. All that Persephone left behind were the scattered flowers she had picked.

Demeter heard the echo of her daughter's cries for help and frantically looked for her everywhere, weeping all the while. While Demeter searched for Persephone, she ignored her duties as the goddess of grains. The neglected crops withered and died, and people starved.

When Demeter learned what had happened to her daughter, she demanded that Hades return Persephone to her. Demeter's neglect caused humans great suffering and sorrow. So Zeus joined Demeter in insisting that Hades release Persephone—but on one condition: that the girl hadn't eaten anything in the Underworld.

Pomegranate

Unfortunately, Persephone had nibbled a few pomegranate seeds given to her by Hades. Zeus and Hades reached a compromise: Persephone would spend most of the year by her mother's side on Earth, and the rest of the year in the Underworld as Hades' wife and queen.

Hades

Persephone

Cerberus

"Who can think about food at a time like this?"

OH, BABY!

Demeter goes undercover as a babysitter, with some fiery results.

While she was searching for Persephone, Demeter disguised herself as an old woman. She was met with kindness by King Celeus and his wife, Metanira. Unaware that the old woman was a goddess, the royal couple invited Demeter to live with them as a nanny for their sons Demophon and Triptolemus.

As a reward for their kindness, Demeter decided that she would make Demophon **immortal**. So each night the goddess breathed gently on the child, coated him with **ambrosia**, and put his body in the fire so that his **mortality** would burn away.

One night Metanira walked into the nursery and screamed in horror at the sight of her baby burning in the fire. With that, the spell was broken, and Demophon was fated to remain a **mortal**. Instead of honoring Demophon, Demeter showed her favor to Triptolemus by teaching him the secrets of agriculture.

ERYSICHTHON'S EMPTINESS

A king offends the goddess and gets really, really hungry.

Erysichthon was a selfish king who made the mistake of offending Demeter. The king needed a new hall for feasts, so he cut down a grove of trees that was sacred to the goddess. In the process, the king killed a **Dryad** who was very special to Demeter. To punish the king, Demeter asked the goddess Aethon to curse Erysichthon. From then on, no matter how much Erysichthon ate, he was always insatiably hungry. He ate all his crops and spent all his money on food and was still desperate for something more to eat. He even sold his own daughter into slavery many times to get more money for food. Erysichthon's entire kingdom was laid waste by his appetite, yet the king was still famished. Finally, Erysichthon began to eat himself—limb by limb—until there was nothing left.

REALITY CHECK

Prader-Willi syndrome is a genetic disease that affects the hypothalamus, a part of the brain that normally registers feeling hunger and fullness. People afflicted with this disease have a continuous and uncontrollable urge to eat.

Want to know more? Go to: www.pwsausa.org

THE ELEUSINIAN MYSTERIES

Top-secret rituals celebrate Demeter and Persephone.

Demeter and Persephone were the central figures behind the Eleusinian Mysteries, secret religious rituals that took place in the village of Eleusis for over two thousand years. Because participants were sworn to secrecy when they were initiated into the cult, only a few facts are known about the Eleusinian Mysteries. It is believed that worshippers were plunged into water and subjected to alternating darkness and light, and that a sacred chest and basket were involved (but no one knows exactly what was hidden inside them). The rites of the Eleusinian Mysteries were designed to symbolize a pattern of death and rebirth, just as the events in the story of Demeter and Persephone symbolize the changing of the seasons and the "death" and "rebirth" of crops.

REALITY CHECK

Famous as both the site of the Eleusinian Mysteries and the birthplace of Greek playwright Aeschylus, modern-day Eleusis is a town north of Athens.

Want to see know more? Go to:
http://homepage.mac.com/cparada/GML/Eleusis.html

Eleusis

> "I'd tell you more, but then they wouldn't be mysteries!"

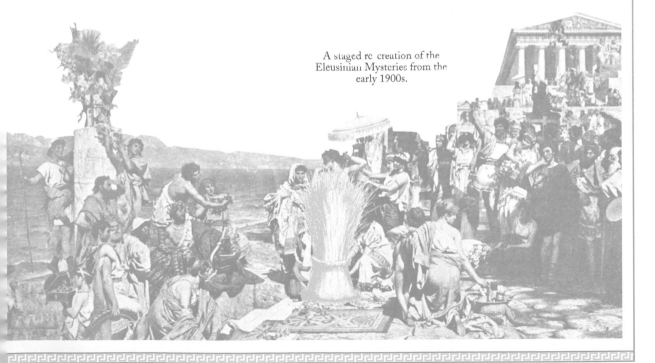

A staged re-creation of the Eleusinian Mysteries from the early 1900s.

Sounds Like: **ee'-ahs**

Roman Name: **Aurora**

Generation: ✓ **Titan**
☐ **Olympian**
☐ **Other**

Divine Powers: **Dawn**

Attributes: **Golden chariot**
Golden robe
Sparkling tiara
White wings

Top 10 Things to Know About Me:

10. I'm called "rosy-fingered dawn" because of the rising sun's fingerlike rays.

9. Aphrodite was in a snit about my fling with Ares, so she cursed me with a longing for handsome young men!

8. I'm my brother's herald. Every morning I race across the sky before Helios to announce his arrival.

7. My son Memnon was killed in the Trojan War.

6. Each night on my way back to my palace, I weep for Memnon; my tears form the morning dew.

5. I begged Zeus to make my beloved Tithonus immortal—but I forgot to request eternal youth for him!

4. My sister, Selene, is the goddess of the moon.

3. Four of my sons, including Boreas and Zephyrus, are gods of the winds.

2. My kids with Astraeus are real stars.

1. I know how to ride in style!

> Rise and shine! Wakey, wakey!

▼ **Family, Flings, Friends, and Foes**

▼ Parents

Hyperion and Theia

▼ Siblings

Helios

Selene

▼ Spouse

Astraeus

▼ Offspring

Boreas

Zephyrus

Notus

Eurus

Emathion

EOS

I'M *SO* IN LOVE!

selene? OMGs, u would not believe the cute guy i met yesterday! BUT FORGET HIM, because at the moment i can't breathe ... the most gorgeous guy EVER just walked by. OMGs, he's totally looking at me ... i am so in love and this time it's 4-real ... his name is tithonus. OH, NO, heart attack! guess what? astraeus just txtd me. he wants 2 see me later. i think he's the 1. oops. gotta run. time 2 get the sun up. txt me.

▼ Flings

Tithonus

Orion

Ares

Cephalus

Cleitus

Ganymede

Memnon

▼ Foes

Aphrodite

Heracles

EOS

"Oh, what a beautiful morning ..."

MYTHLOPEDIA

Ηως

IT'S GREEK TO ME

Eos was the goddess of the dawn, as well as the **personification** of the dawn. Personification, or giving human characteristics to a non-human thing, is a common theme in Greek mythology. In fact, Eos's rosy fingers are a perfect example of personification. The pink rays of the sun at dawn reminded ancient Greeks of fingers, which is how Eos ended up with the nickname rosy fingers.

> "Aiming high and shining bright runs in the family!"

SUN AND MOON SIBS

Eos has a heavenly heritage. Eos came from a stellar family. Her parents were the Titans Hyperion, the god of light, and Theia. Eos's siblings included Helios, god of the sun, and Selene, goddess of the moon. In addition to being **deities**, all three siblings were also personifications of natural **phenomena**.

Eos, the Dawn, heralded the rise of Helios, who pulled the sun across the sky in his golden **chariot**. While Helios sailed back to the east, Selene, the Moon, appeared as day faded into night. These three were responsible for the cyclical passage of day into night, and then the start of each new day.

Selene

Helios

HERE COMES THE SUN

Sun's up! Eos heralds her brother's arrival.

As the goddess of the dawn, Eos served as **herald** for her brother Helios, the god of the sun. At the end of each night, Eos would rise out of the east and wave away the darkness with her rosy fingers, making way for the sun. Some stories say that she flew through the sky on her own pair of wings, spreading light. Other stories say that she had her own golden chariot, which she drove across the sky. Still others claim that Eos rode across the sky on the winged horse Pegasus. Helios followed Eos, towing the sun across the sky with his golden chariot.

THE CURSE OF APHRODITE

The love goddess curses Eos with a desire for handsome young men.

Eos was busy as the goddess of the dawn, but not too busy for romance! The gorgeous goddess was completely crazy about handsome young men.

Although Eos was an attractive and alluring goddess, there was more—or less—to her love affairs than mutual affection. Eos's very first boyfriend was Ares, the god of war, who was also adored by Aphrodite, the goddess of love. When Aphrodite discovered their romance, she cursed Eos with a longing for handsome young men. As a result of this curse, Eos fell madly in love with such young cuties as Tithonus, Cephalus, Cleitus, Orion, and Ganymede.

Hey, Eos, keep your rosy fingers off my boyfriend!

Aphrodite

"Everybody up! It's a new day!"

Helios

Eos

GODDESS MAGAZINE QUIZ

WHAT'S YOUR ♥ STYLE?

Name: *Eos*

1. You like guys who are:
   a) handsome
   b) young
   c) **handsome and young** ✓

2. Your favorite way to spend an afternoon is:
   a) curled up with a good book
   b) spending time with your best friends
   c) **spending time curled up with a handsome young guy** ✓

3. Your dream date would be:
   a) a candlelight dinner
   b) a wild party
   c) **a wild candlelight dinner with a handsome young guy** ✓

4. You can't resist:
   a) a giant brownie
   b) a slice of pizza
   c) **eating brownies and pizza with a handsome young guy** ✓

Scoring : If you answered mostly Cs, look out! You may have been cursed by the goddess of love!

THE TROUBLE WITH TITHONUS

Eos makes a request but leaves out an important detail.

Eos fell in love with Tithonus, the handsome young prince of Troy. She invited him to her palace, along with Ganymede, another gorgeous young man. But when the mighty god Zeus saw Ganymede, he insisted that the boy leave Eos's palace for Mount Olympus, where he became Zeus's **cupbearer**. Eos agreed to let Ganymede go to Zeus, but she made a request of her own: that Zeus gift her lover Tithonus with **immortality**. Unfortunately, Eos forgot to ask Zeus to grant eternal youth for Tithonus. So Tithonus lived forever, aging as the years passed. Eventually Tithonus became a wrinkled, stooped old man, who shuffled around the palace halls. Eos grew so tired of the old man's failing memory and constant chattering that she locked him in a room. When he was finally too old and weak to get out of bed— yet wouldn't stop babbling—Eos turned him into a cicada.

REALITY CHECK

Cicadas are medium- to large-size insects that live in trees. In summer, the males make a loud, almost deafening buzzing noise. Cicada nymphs typically live underground for 17 years before emerging as adults. But their adulthood is brief, lasting a mere 30 to 40 days.

Want to know more? Go to:
http://www.cicadamania.com/cicadas/

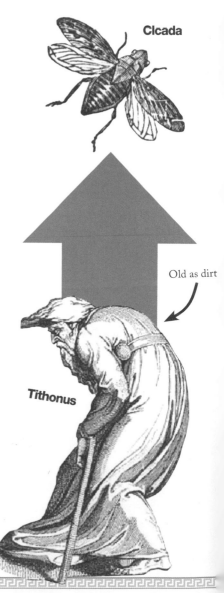

Cicada

Old as dirt

Tithonus

MOM OF MILLIONS

Eos's large family includes the four winds and all the stars.

Eos not only had many men in her life—she also had many children. She and Tithonus had two sons, Emathion and Memnon. Emathion grew up to become the king of Ethiopia. He was later killed by the mighty hero Heracles. Memnon had a similar destiny—first serving as a king of Ethiopia, then dying at the hand of Achilles during the Trojan War.

Eos and her husband, Astraeus, were the parents of the four winds—Boreas, the wintry north wind; Zephyrus, the warm west wind; Eurus, the east wind; and Notus, the south wind. Eos and Astraeus also populated the sky with stars—millions of them!

Eos

> "Most of my kids were stars— real stars!"

MOURNING DEW

Each night, Eos cries tears of sorrow.

When Eos's son Memnon was brutally killed by the hero Achilles in the Trojan War, the goddess was devastated. Each night, on her journey from the west to the east to prepare for the start of a new dawn, Eos wept bitterly, overwhelmed by grief. Her tears settled all over the earth, forming the dew that glints and glitters in the morning sunlight.

REALITY CHECK

Dew is atmospheric moisture that condenses on objects, usually at night. The ground dampness formed when a warm, moist wind blows over cold earth is also called dew.

Eos

Memnon

Dewdrops

▼ Profile of The Fates

Sounds Like: **Kloh'-tho, Lack'-uh-siss At'-roe-poss**

Roman Name: **the Parcae**

Greek Name: **the Moirai**

Generation: ☐ Titan
☑ Olympian
☑ Other

Divine Powers: **Spinning the thread of life**
Assigning a length to each mortal life
Cutting the thread of life
Determining one's destiny

Attributtes: **Globe**
Scissors
Scroll
Spindle
White robes

Top 10 Things to Know About Us:

10. Our parents are Zeus, the ruler of the gods, and Themis, goddess of justice.

9. We decide how long mortals will live—and what their destinies will be. You might want to give us extra nice presents!

8. Clotho, the Spinner, spins the thread of life.

7. Lachesis, the Assigner of Lots, decides how long the thread—the person's life—should be.

6. Atropos, the Unbending One, cuts the thread to end life.

5. We hang out with Eileithyia, the goddess of childbirth, since we're present at every baby's birth.

4. We tell the Furies whom to punish—and why.

3. We've been described as cold, unfeeling, and ugly old women. That really hurts our feelings!

2. Even the gods are afraid of us—we have power over their destinies, too.

1. Some of the greatest prophecies of ancient times came from us.

I can't find my tape measure ...

Who took my string?

Has anybody see my scissors?

▼ Family, Flings, Friends, and Foes

▼ Parents

Zeus and Themis

▼ Siblings

The Hours

▼ Foes

Apollo   **Meleager**   **Althaea**   **Typhon**

The FATES

1-555-GOT-FATE

Questions about your future? Wondering if that special someone has a wandering eye? Curious about the time and place of your death? Then don't delay—call 1-555-GOT-FATE! We were present at the moment of your birth and have already determined every single thing, good and bad, that will happen to you! Atropos is standing by with her scissors, possibly about to cut *your* thread of life, and you deserve to know! First minute costs 99 drachmas, each additional minute, 85 drachmas. Call now, before it's too late!

Ouija Board

The FATES

"If we could turn back time ..."

MYTH LOPEDIA

IT'S GREEK TO ME

The Fates weren't just goddesses of destiny, they actually were destiny. The concept of destiny—that events in an individual's life are unavoidable—was an important one to the Greeks. No wonder they needed three goddesses to handle it!

DESIGNERS OF DESTINY

The Fates know what's coming.

Three sisters—Clotho, Lachesis, and Atropos—were known as the Fates. These goddesses were vitally important and frighteningly powerful. Some stories say that even almighty Zeus was afraid of the Fates and their ability to influence the course of events. But other stories say that Zeus was really the god in control, and the Fates just carried out his orders.

Dressed in white robes, these ugly old women together determined the destiny of **mortals**' lives. The Fates were present at the birth of every baby. Clotho, the Spinner, would spin the thread that represented the baby's life. Lachesis, the Assigner of **Lots**, stood nearby with her measuring stick to determine the length of the thread (and the baby's life). Atropos, the Unbending One, was the most powerful—and the most feared. She had a pair of shears ready to cut the thread of life, thereby bringing death. Together, the three sisters determined every aspect of a person's life, doling out both good and bad so there would be balance.

"Want to know your fate? Are you sure?"

Clotho   Lachesis   Atropos

MELEAGER'S MOTHER

A mother tries to escape the Fates—but plays right into their hands.

When Althaea gave birth to her son Meleager, she wanted nothing but the best for her newborn boy. She was horrified to hear Atropos, the Fate who determined when a person would die, declare that Meleager would live only until a log then in the fireplace had completely burned to ash.

Desperate to save her son, Althaea snatched the burning log out of the fire and extinguished it; then she wrapped it carefully and hid it in a safe place.

Spared an early death, Meleager grew into a brave and valiant young man. Thanks to his mother, he had evaded the fate Atropos had decided for him ... or so it seemed. Then, one fateful day, Meleager had an argument with his uncles. It turned violent, and he ended up killing them. Althaea was furious at her son and heartbroken about the deaths of her brothers. In a rage, she retrieved the log she had stowed away since Meleager's birth, and threw it into the fire. Meleager, his fate sealed, died in agony.

A TRICK ON TYPHON

Zeus defeats a horrible monster—with a little help from the Fates.

Typhon was a hideous and terrifying monster. This huge beast had one hundred heads and eyes that dripped venom, and he breathed fire. Even the gods feared him!

Typhon believed he was entitled to rule heaven and earth, so he challenged the Olympian gods and tried to seize control from Zeus. But the Fates had already determined that Zeus was going to win. To make sure that Zeus would beat Typhon, they told the monster that if he ate a special fruit, he would grow even more powerful. Typhon, of course, gobbled the fruit with glee, but it actually made him weaker. He tried to throw Mount Etna at the gods, but Zeus fought back with his powerful thunderbolts. The thunderbolts made the mountain land right on top of

Typhon, burying the vicious beast—and ensuring that Zeus would prevail as the ruler of Olympus! Typhon remains trapped beneath Mount Etna to this day.

> "Here, Typhon! Want some fruit salad?"

REALITY CHECK

The mountain that landed on Typhon (according to legend) is now the highest active volcano in Europe, Mount Etna in Sicily. Its ancient Greek name was Aitne. Rising more than eleven thousand feet, it has been erupting lava for more than eight thousand years!

Want to know more? Go to:
http://www.bestofsicily.com/etna.htm

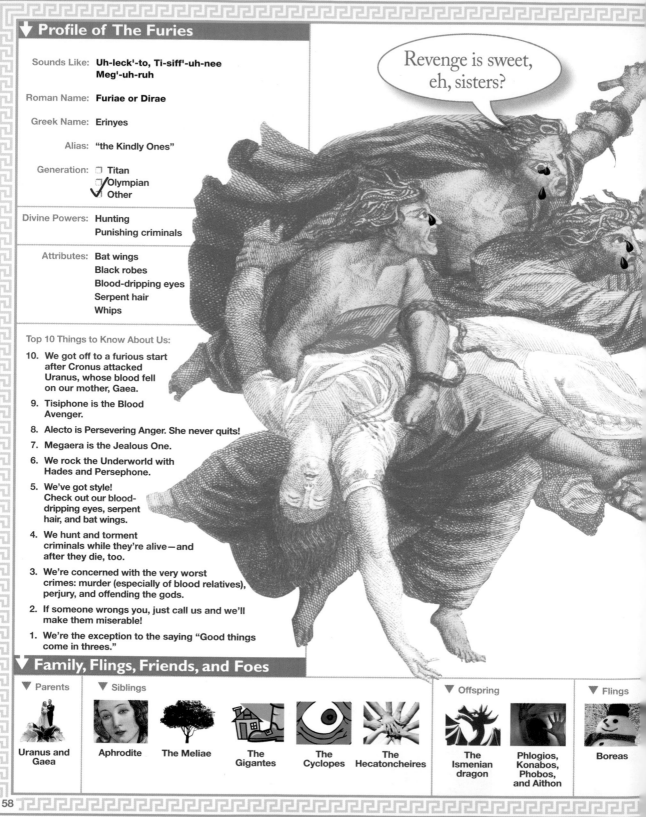

Profile of The Furies

Sounds Like: Uh-leck'-to, Ti-siff'-uh-nee Meg'-uh-ruh

Roman Name: Furiae or Dirae

Greek Name: Erinyes

Alias: "the Kindly Ones"

Generation: ☐ Titan
☐ Olympian
☑ Other

Divine Powers: Hunting
Punishing criminals

Attributes: Bat wings
Black robes
Blood-dripping eyes
Serpent hair
Whips

Top 10 Things to Know About Us:

10. We got off to a furious start after Cronus attacked Uranus, whose blood fell on our mother, Gaea.

9. Tisiphone is the Blood Avenger.

8. Alecto is Persevering Anger. She never quits!

7. Megaera is the Jealous One.

6. We rock the Underworld with Hades and Persephone.

5. We've got style! Check out our blood-dripping eyes, serpent hair, and bat wings.

4. We hunt and torment criminals while they're alive—and after they die, too.

3. We're concerned with the very worst crimes: murder (especially of blood relatives), perjury, and offending the gods.

2. If someone wrongs you, just call us and we'll make them miserable!

1. We're the exception to the saying "Good things come in threes."

Revenge is sweet, eh, sisters?

Family, Flings, Friends, and Foes

▼ Parents

Uranus and Gaea

▼ Siblings

Aphrodite

The Meliae

The Gigantes

The Cyclopes

The Hecatoncheires

▼ Offspring

The Ismenian dragon

Phlogios, Konabos, Phobos, and Aithon

▼ Flings

Boreas

The FURIES

BOUNTY HUNTERS

Excitement! Adventure! Revenge! Tune in this fall for all-new episodes of BOUNTY HUNTERS! Follow along with three tough goddesses, the Furies, as they hunt and haunt the worst criminals—and make them pay for their crimes! From the depths of the Underworld to the peaks of Mount Olympus, these hideous hags do what's necessary for justice to be served. Starring Tisiphone, the Blood Avenger; Alecto, Persevering Anger; and Megaera, the Jealous One. Viewer discretion is advised.

Oedipus

Chill out, ladies!

REALITY CHECK

The image below depicts the Furies tormenting a victim. It's from a vase in the collection of the British Museum, and dates to about 330 BCE.

Want to know more? Go to. http://www.artfund.org/ artwork/240/greek-vase- orestes-pursued-by-the-furies

▼ Friends

Ares

Nemesis

Nike

Hades

Persephone

▼ Foes

Athena

Apollo

Orestes

Oedipus

Ερινυες

The FURIES

"One way or another, we're gonna find you!"

MYTH LOPEDIA

IT'S GREEK TO ME

Three Furies, three Fates: the number three is *everywhere* in Greek mythology, from the three Gorgons to the three Graces. Even Cerberus, the watchdog of the **Underworld**, had three heads! Numbers that are favored in a culture or society are known as pattern numbers.

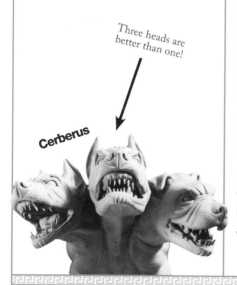

Three heads are better than one!

Cerberus

THE ORIGINAL AVENGERS

Criminals, beware! The Furies will hunt you and haunt you.

The Furies, three sisters whose role was to pursue and punish criminals, were the offspring of Gaea (Earth) and Uranus (Sky). The Furies sought **retribution** for the very worst crimes: murder, **perjury**, disrespect to family, and offending a god or goddess. The Furies' violent family history (Uranus was attacked by his son Cronus) is especially fitting since one of the crimes they **avenged** was violence against a blood relative. As for their looks: UGH! The three Furies were grotesque flying women, with bat wings, serpents for hair, and eyes that dripped blood.

The sisters included
- **Tisiphone**, who sought revenge for murder;
- **Alecto**, whose anger never ceased;
- **Megaera**, who was known for her jealousy.

Some stories say there was a whole host of Furies who were led by Tisiphone, Alecto, and Megaera. Typically the Furies would pursue a criminal until he or she went insane and died.

REALITY CHECK

The 2003 film *Charlie's Angels: Full Throttle* featured three modern-day female criminal hunters. The movie was a sequel to the 2000 *Charlie's Angels*; both were based on a television series that ran from 1976 to 1981.

Want to know more? Go to:
http://www.sonypictures.com/homevideo/charliesangels/

Orestes

Furies

THE HUNTING OF ORESTES

A hero gets sucked into his family's murderous schemes and pays a painful price.

The Greek hero Orestes was hunted by the Furies. His mother, Clytemnestra, had murdered his father, Agamemnon, a Trojan war hero. To avenge his father's death, Orestes killed Clytemnestra and her boyfriend. To the Furies, the murder of a family member was among the worst crimes. So they relentlessly pursued Orestes for killing his mother, tracking him by smelling the air for the scent of Clytemnestra's blood. Finally, Orestes begged for help from Apollo and Athena. Orestes was put on trial for Clytemnestra's murder and **acquitted**, thanks to Athena's intervention. The goddess claimed that he had suffered enough torment from the Furies. The Furies were outraged that Athena would interfere with their punishment, but she eventually calmed them down.

REALITY CHECK

The bloodhound is a breed of hound in the sporting group of dogs that dates to the eighth century. Bloodhounds have the keenest sense of smell of any dog. Like the Furies, they can recognize and follow, or track, a human scent over long distances.

Want to know more? Go to: www.bloodhounds.org

"You can run, but you can't hide!"

Bloodhound

THE TORMENT OF OEDIPUS

Oedipus pays dearly for his accidental crimes.

When Oedipus was born, it was foretold that he would grow up to murder his father, Laius, and marry his mother, Jocasta. Jocasta was desperate to avoid the **prophecy** so she asked a shepherd to leave her baby in a meadow to die. The kindly shepherd couldn't bring himself to do it. Instead he gave Oedipus to a childless couple, King Polybus and Queen Periboea.

Things were going well until Oedipus heard about the prophecy. Believing that his adoptive parents were his birth parents, Oedipus ran away. While traveling, he encountered an older man with four attendants. When the men tried to force Oedipus from the road, he refused to move. A fight erupted and Oedipus killed the man and three of his companions. He did not know that the man he'd killed was his birth father, King Laius.

Later Oedipus met Jocasta, who was now a widow. Not realizing she was his birth mother, Oedipus married her and became king of Thebes. This outraged the Furies, who punished Oedipus by bringing plague and famine to the city of Thebes.

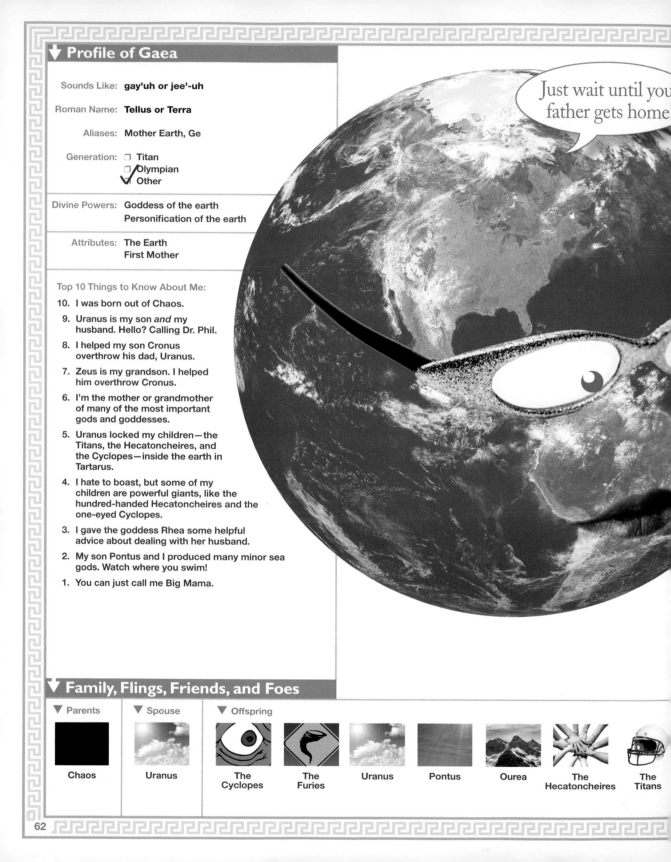

▼ Profile of Gaea

Sounds Like: **gay'uh or jee'-uh**

Roman Name: **Tellus or Terra**

Aliases: **Mother Earth, Ge**

Generation: ☐ Titan
☐ Olympian
☑ Other

Divine Powers: **Goddess of the earth**
Personification of the earth

Attributes: **The Earth**
First Mother

Top 10 Things to Know About Me:

10. I was born out of Chaos.

9. Uranus is my son *and* my husband. Hello? Calling Dr. Phil.

8. I helped my son Cronus overthrow his dad, Uranus.

7. Zeus is my grandson. I helped him overthrow Cronus.

6. I'm the mother or grandmother of many of the most important gods and goddesses.

5. Uranus locked my children—the Titans, the Hecatoncheires, and the Cyclopes—inside the earth in Tartarus.

4. I hate to boast, but some of my children are powerful giants, like the hundred-handed Hecatoncheires and the one-eyed Cyclopes.

3. I gave the goddess Rhea some helpful advice about dealing with her husband.

2. My son Pontus and I produced many minor sea gods. Watch where you swim!

1. You can just call me Big Mama.

Just wait until you father gets home!

▼ Family, Flings, Friends, and Foes

▼ Parents	▼ Spouse	▼ Offspring						
Chaos	Uranus	The Cyclopes	The Furies	Uranus	Pontus	Ourea	The Hecatoncheires	The Titans

GAEA

MOTHER OF THE YEAR ... OR NOT

What in the *world* is going on here? I step out for one minute and you kids go wild! Cyclopes, you're grounded! Not another one-eyed staring contest until you clean your cave! Hecatoncheires, keep your hundred hands to yourselves! And as for you Titans, I've had it with your roughhousing—you've trampled my begonias for the last time! Your father will be home soon and nothing makes him madder than when you kids mess around. Don't upset him or you'll be sorry!

> Mom, he's staring at me!

Cyclopes

REALITY CHECK

Since 1969, Earth Day has been celebrated annually on April 22 to focus attention on the protection and conservation of natural resources. Now international in scope, Earth Day honors the environment and reminds humankind of the importance of environmental protection.

Want to know more? Go to: http://www.earthday.net/

			▼ Flings	▼ Friends	▼ Foes	
Sea Gods	The Gigantes	Typhon	Tartarus	Eros	Cronus	Uranus

63

"Mother knows best!"

MYTHLOPEDIA

Γαια

IT'S GREEK TO ME

According to Greek myth, the universe (cosmos) began with **Chaos**, a vast, empty space for everything to fit in. It was followed by Earth (Gaea), a world for gods and humans; Tartarus, an underworld for defeated **immortals**; and Love (Eros), a force of attraction that drew living beings together to mate with one another, producing nearly everything in the world.

In this myth, most elements in the cosmos are living beings who belong to a single great family. Nonhuman elements are treated as though they have human qualities. This practice is known as **personification**.

THE ORIGINAL EARTH MOTHER

Just your average mom, Gaea makes order out of Chaos and populates the earth.

Gaea had many kids—a whole lot of kids! She gave birth to Uranus, the sky; Ourea, the mountains; and Pontus, the sea. Together Gaea and Uranus began to populate the world. Their children included the Hecatoncheires, massive giants with one hundred hands each; the Gigantes; and the three Cyclopes, who were one-eyed giants. Gaea and Uranus's

offspring also included the Furies, Aphrodite, and the Titans, the twelve **deities** who preceded the Olympians. With Pontus (the sea), Gaea produced numerous sea gods, and with Tartarus (deepest realm of the **Underworld**), she produced the monster Typhon. But that's not all. According to some stories, she was also the force that gave life to animals and birds—and even some humans!

Cyclopes

LOOK OUT, URANUS

A paranoid pop imprisons his offspring—and mama gets revenge!

Gaea and Uranus's Titan kids were unusual, to say the least. In fact, Uranus found himself increasingly fearful of the Titans he had fathered; he was afraid that they would be able to overpower him. So to get his children out of the way, Uranus imprisoned them in Tartarus, which was located inside the earth—deep within Gaea herself.

Having living beings locked inside her caused Gaea tremendous pain. Finally she couldn't take it anymore. She convinced her sons to attack Uranus so that they could be free.

One night, the youngest Titan, Cronus, attacked Uranus with a sickle that Gaea had provided. Wounded, Uranus limped away. After the Titans were released from Tartarus, the era of their rule began, with Cronus as their leader.

LIKE FATHER, LIKE SON

Cronus follows in his dad's footsteps.

After Cronus became the ruler of the Titans, he and his sister Rhea started a family. But when Gaea and Uranus predicted that Cronus would be overthrown by his own son, Cronus became just as afraid of his children as Uranus had been.

To avoid the fulfillment of the **prophecy**, Cronus decided to get rid of his children! So as each of his babies was born—Hestia, Hera, Hades, Demeter, and Poseidon—Cronus swallowed them whole, one by one! Rhea was desperate as she watched Cronus gulp down each baby, and she begged Gaea to help. Gaea told Rhea to wrap a stone in a baby blanket and present it to Cronus the next time she gave birth—then to take the real baby and hide it someplace safe. When Rhea gave birth to baby Zeus, she followed Gaea's advice. Cronus popped the blanket-wrapped stone into his mouth and swallowed, not suspecting a thing.

When Zeus was grown, he gave Cronus a **potion** to make him vomit. Out spewed Zeus's brothers and sisters. Finally the Olympians were free—and ready to challenge the Titans to a battle for ultimate power.

REALITY CHECK

Under stress, mother hamsters have been known to eat their babies (Cronus only swallowed his). But their usual diet consists of seeds, grains, fruits, and vegetables.

Want to know more? Go to:
http://www.aspca.org/pet-care/small-pet-care/hamster-care.html

"Cronus, I raised you better than this!"

Zeus made his dad drink up.

Profile of The Graces

Sounds Like: **Thu-lie'-uh, Yoo-fross'-i-nee, U-glee'-uh**

Roman Name: **Gratiae**

Greek Name: **Charites**

Generation: ☐ Titan
☐ Olympian
☑ Other

Divine Powers: Beauty
Charm
Grace

Attributes: Apollo's lyre
Myrtle

Top 10 Things to Know About Us:

10. We started out as goddesses of fertility and nature, but our identities changed over time.

9. We're in tight with our gal pals the Muses.

8. Artists always show the three of us together, often dancing to the music of Apollo's lyre.

7. Thalia is the Grace of bloom and beauty.

6. Euphrosyne is the Grace of joy and festivity.

5. Aglaia is the Grace of splendor and brilliance.

4. We bring grace, charm, and beauty to the affairs of gods and mortals.

3. We're sources of great inspiration to mortals, especially in the areas of poetry, music, and art.

2. The Charitesia was a festival that celebrated us, with lots of music and dance.

1. We're BFFs with Aphrodite; we go everywhere together!

> We'd like to thank all the little people ...

Family, Flings, Friends, and Foes

▼ **Parents**

Zeus and Eurynome

▼ **Flings**

Hephaestus

▼ **Friends**

Aphrodite

Hera

Apollo

Athena

Eros

Dionysus

The Muses

The GRACES

THANK US? NO, THANK *YOU!*

Dear Mortals,

Thank you ever so much for your worship. Your praise is greatly appreciated; it is our distinct pleasure to grace your feasts with our charm and beauty. Why, just the other day we told Apollo that the mortals had simply outdone themselves with their plans for the Charitesia! Words simply cannot express how humbled we are by such a magnificent feast held in our honor. You are too kind!

Sincerely yours,

The Graces

Aphrodite

Good afternoon, ladies!

67

Χαριτες

The GRACES

"Aren't we lovely ...?"

MYTHOPEDIA

IT'S GREEK TO ME

Greek mythology is chock-full of divine guilds: groups of siblings who worked together at the same jobs. Most divine guilds had three members, and were more often made up of sisters than brothers. The Graces are a perfect example of a divine guild—three sisters working together for a common purpose. Other examples of divine guilds include the Furies and the Fates.

"Charmed, we're sure!"

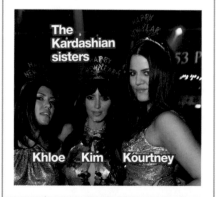

The Kardashian sisters

Khloe Kim Kourtney

MEET THE GRACES

The Graces keep things pretty, witty, and bright.

Euphrosyne, Thalia, and Aglaia were known as the Graces, divine **personifications** of charm and beauty. The Graces were rarely separated. Their combined forces brought beauty and charm to the events of gods and **mortals**. Euphrosyne was the Grace of joy and festivity. Thalia was the Grace of bloom and beauty. Aglaia, the youngest, was the Grace of splendor and brilliance. They often accompanied Aphrodite, the goddess of love, who had a special fondness for beautiful things. As part of their duties, the Graces inspired sculptors, musicians, poets, dancers, and public speakers—especially at happy events.

The Graces

CONFUSED WITH THE MUSES?

The Graces and the Muses aren't so different after all.

The Muses were nine goddesses of poetry, music, dance, and artistic, intellectual, and scientific pursuits. Their primary duties were to offer inspiration in their special fields—which sounds a lot like the role of the Graces. In fact, there was much overlap between the Graces and the Muses, so much so that their stories often intertwined. The Muses and the Graces lived together on Mount Olympus, and both groups served Aphrodite, the goddess of love, as attendants. The Muses played a larger role in inspiring artists, while the Graces helped translate that inspiration into actual creative work.

The Graces

Aglaia	splendor, brilliance
Euphrosyne	joy, festivity
Thalia	bloom, beauty

The Muses

Calliope	epic and heroic poetry
Clio	history
Erato	lyric and love poetry
Euterpe	music
Melpomene	tragic poetry
Polyhymnia	sacred poetry and hymns
Terpsichore	dance, choral poetry, and song
Thalia	comic poetry and rural life
Urania	astronomy

CHARM AT THE CHARITESIA

A festival to celebrate the Graces is very charming.

An ancient shrine at Orchomenus was the site of the Charitesia, a special festival that honored the Graces. The Charitesia included music and dance, as well as contests in music and poetry. Aphrodite may also have been celebrated at the Charitesia because of her close friendship with the Graces. After all, even the goddess of love is inspired by charm and beauty!

"Those mortals are the most gracious hosts!"

REALITY CHECK

In 1922, Emily Post published *Etiquette: The Blue Book of Social Usage*. It explains the rules of social conduct, or graces, such as how to write a thank-you note and which fork to use at a fancy dinner party. Today, the Emily Post Institute's Web site offers tips for teens on online friending and cell-phone manners.

Want to know more? Go to: http://www.emilypost.com/

▼ Profile of Hebe

Sounds Like: **hee'-bee**

Roman Name: **Juventas**

Aliases: Ganymeda, Dia

Generation:
- ☐ Titan
- ☑ Olympian
- ☐ Other

Divine Powers: **Brides**
Youth

Attributes: **Cup**
Pitcher

Age is a state of mind!

Top 10 Things to Know About Me:

10. As handmaiden to the Olympians, I serve them nectar and ambrosia. Care for a snack?

9. I help my mom, Hera, get into and out of her chariot.

8. I draw baths for my brother Ares, and help him get dressed—he may be the god of war but he's still my baby bro.

7. After I married Heracles, Ganymede got my job as cupbearer to the gods— that's why Ganymeda is one of my names.

6. I'm the goddess of brides.

5. My mom, Hera, tormented Heracles—until I married him.

4. I can make old people young again.

3. People worship me, hoping that I'll make them younger or more beautiful.

2. I'm able to grant immortality. It pays to be really nice to me!

1. I granted elderly Iolaus one day of youth so he could battle Eurystheus.

▼ Family, Flings, Friends, and Foes

▼ Parents	▼ Siblings		▼ Spouse	▼ Flings		▼ Friends
Zeus and Hera	Ares	Eileithyia	Heracles	Alexiares	Anicetus	Aphrodite

HEBE
FOUNTAIN OF YOUTH

Saggy skin? Wrinkly face? Gray hair? Kiss signs of aging good-bye with Hebe's Forever Young Lifestyle Program! Worship your way to youth and be as beautiful as you deserve to be (just follow in my footsteps). Private consultations available—I'll pour the nectar; you listen to tales of my heroic husband, Heracles, as we discuss personalized ways to maximize your youthful beauty—while you've still got it!

Iolaus

Ganymede   **Eurystheus**

Please? Just one sip?

HEBE

"When you look good, you feel good."

MYTH LOPEDIA

IT'S GREEK TO ME

The young and beautiful goddess of youth was celebrated with festivals that were known for nonstop fun! A major center of Hebe's worship was located in Athens, not far from an area where Heracles, Hebe's husband, was worshipped. There was also a temple dedicated to Hebe in Sicyon, and a sacred group of trees dedicated to her in Phlius.

Hebe

FOREVER YOUNG

A goddess shares the secret for eternal youth.

Hebe, a daughter of the mighty god Zeus and his wife, Hera, was the goddess of eternal youth, as well as the **personification** of youth. She was also the handmaiden of the gods. She poured them **nectar** and served **ambrosia**, which they drank and ate to remain forever young. She was worshipped by **mortals** because it was believed that she could restore youthful beauty to the aged. In Rome, where she was known as Juventas, she was the patron of young manhood.

REALITY CHECK

According to legend, Spanish explorer Juan Ponce de Leon landed in Saint Augustine, Florida, in 1513, searching for the Fountain of Youth.

Want to know more? Go to:
www.fountainofyouthflorida.com

"Looking young comes naturally to me!"

Hebe

YOUNG AT HEART
An old warrior longs for one more day of youth.

One fascinating myth about Hebe involves Heracles' nephew Iolaus. When King Eurystheus, an old foe of Heracles, threatened Heracles' children, Heracles requested that Hebe make Iolaus young again; he wanted his nephew to battle Eurystheus. Heracles, ever the hero, would have fought Eurystheus himself—except he had already been brought to live on Mount Olympus as Hebe's husband.

Hebe did not want to use her power to interfere with the natural order of life. But Themis, the goddess of divine justice, assured Hebe that it was right for her to help Iolaus in this way. So Hebe obliged and Iolaus enjoyed one more day of youth in his old age. He charged into battle as a healthy young man—and captured Eurystheus, ensuring that Heracles' children would be safe.

REALITY CHECK
According to the Worldwatch Institute, Americans spend about $8 billion on cosmetics each year. If Hebe could still help mortals stay young, she'd be very busy!

Want to know more? Go to:
http://www.worldwatch.org/node/764

A NIP OF NECTAR
A handmaiden's work is never done.

In addition to her role as the goddess of eternal youth, Hebe was the handmaiden of the gods. As handmaiden, she assisted the important Olympians with their daily lives. For example, she prepared the bath for her brother Ares and helped him get dressed. She helped her mother, Hera, as she got in and out of her **chariot.** Hebe also served as the gods' **cupbearer.** She carried a special pitcher that contained fragrant and delicious nectar, a special drink that provided **Immortality** to those who drank it. That's why it was reserved for only the gods. After Hebe married Heracles, she stepped down from her role as cupbearer and was replaced by a handsome young man, Ganymede.

HEBE'S HUSBAND, HERACLES
A happy goddess quits her day job.

Heracles, perhaps the most famous of all the Greek heroes, was the son of Zeus and the mortal Alcmene. When Hera, Zeus's wife and Hebe's mother, found out that her husband had a son with another woman, she vowed to ruin Heracles. Hera arranged for Heracles to spend much of his life performing twelve labors, nearly impossible tasks that would have destroyed anyone else. But Heracles, with his extreme strength and impressive intellect, successfully completed each labor. After Heracles died, he was rewarded with immortality, and allowed to ascend to Mount Olympus as a god. He then married Hebe and together they had two sons, Alexiares and Anicetus. When Heracles became Hera's son-in-law and father of her grandsons, she stopped tormenting him.

6:00 AM—up with Eos. Busy day ahead!

7:00 AM—get water for Ares' bath.

8:00 AM—kindle fire to heat water (thank Hestia for help!).

9:00 AM—help Ares take a bath (and boy, does he need one!).

10:00 AM—dress Ares (oof—armor is heavy!).

11:00 AM—warm up Mom's chariot.

12:00 PM—lunchtime. Serve nectar to everybody.

2:00 PM—get more nectar ready for dinner.

3:00 PM— clean up Olympus. This place is a pigsty!

5:00 PM—dinnertime. Pour more nectar for everybody. Again.

8:00 PM—thank gods Selene is rising! I'm exhausted!

▼ Profile of Hera

Sounds Like: hir'-uh

Roman Name: Juno

Generation:
- ☐ Titan
- ☑ Olympian
- ☐ Other

Divine Powers: Childbirth
Marriage
Women

Attributes:
Apple	Hawk
Cow	Lion
Crow	Peacock
Crown	Pomegranate
Cuckoo	Staff tipped with lotus
Gold sandals	Veil

> Where have you been?!?

Top 10 Things to Know About Me:

10. I'm married to Zeus, which makes me queen of the gods.

9. I may be the goddess of marriage but I can't seem to keep my hubby at home.

8. If you mess with my man, you'll get what you deserve. Watch your backs, Leto, Semele, and Io!

7. And as for you little stepsons and stepdaughters, I'll get you, too. Hear me, Dionysus, Heracles, Apollo, Artemis …?

6. Take my advice: You don't want to challenge the mightiest god on Mount Olympus!

5. My son Hephaestus was such an ugly baby that I threw him off Mount Olympus! Does that make me a bad mother?

4. My servant Argus had one hundred eyes; when he died I placed his eyes in the peacock's tail.

3. I blinded the prophet Tiresias for taking Zeus's side in an argument.

2. I helped the Greeks during the Trojan War because Paris, prince of Troy, said Aphrodite was prettier than I am.

1. Iris, the goddess of the rainbow, delivers all my messages.

▼ Family, Flings, Friends, and Foes

▼ Parents	▼ Siblings					▼ Spouse	▼ Offspring	
Cronus and Rhea	Zeus	Poseidon	Hades	Demeter	Hestia	Zeus	Ares	Hephaest

HERA
WATCH YOUR BACK

Is that my husband you're hiding? No? Then you won't mind if I take a peek. AH-HA! Oh. Guess no one's here after all—but I'm sure you don't mind me looking for my husband under the bed. AH-HA! Oh. Just dust bunnies! Was that a noise in the closet? My husband, perhaps? AH-HA! Oh. Nothing but robes and jewels … so many robes and jewels … Are they gifts from my husband? No? Prove it! AH-HA! You're in trouble now, girlfriend!

Zeus

Honey, she's just a friend, honest!

▼ Friends

Eileithyia

The Hesperides

Argus

Iris

▼ Foes

Heracles

Paris

Aphrodite

Leto

Echo

Ηρα

HERA

"One way or another, I'm gonna get you."

MYTHLOPEDIA

IT'S GREEK TO ME

The Greek gods could transform themselves into animals—or even people! When Hera wanted to get even with Semele, one of Zeus's girlfriends, she turned herself into Semele's former nurse. Zeus was notorious for taking on other identities to hide his romances from Hera. He **transformed** himself into a swan, a bull, and even a cloud! The gods also used transformation as a punishment. Athena turned Arachne into a spider for bragging that she was a better weaver than the goddess, and Artemis turned Callisto into a bear for having Zeus as a boyfriend.

Swan

CUCKOO FOR ZEUS

Hera cuddles a cuckoo—and ends up queen of the gods!

Hera was a stunningly beautiful goddess. Not surprisingly, the mighty Zeus, the ruler of the gods and Hera's brother, decided that she would be the perfect wife and queen for him. But Hera was not interested in any sort of romantic entanglement with her brother, and she rejected him.

Zeus, not one to take no for an answer, transformed himself into a **bedraggled** cuckoo bird.

Hera felt sorry for the little bird, and tenderly held it close. Suddenly Hera found herself holding Zeus! The goddess couldn't escape from the mighty god, and she was forced to accept his hand in marriage.

REALITY CHECK

A female European cuckoo will lay an egg in a nest that belongs to a bird of a different species. That bird either leaves her nest or hatches the cuckoo's egg. Tricky birds, those cuckoos!

Want to know more? Go to: http://www.enchantedlearning.com/subjects/birds/info/Cuckoo.shtml

I'm cuckoo for Hera!

Zeus

THERE'S NO FURY LIKE A GODDESS SCORNED

Hera leads a revolt to overthrow Zeus.

During the early days of Zeus's rule on Olympus, many of the Olympians were unhappy with his behavior—especially Hera, who was outraged by Zeus's frequent romances with other **deities**, and even **mortals**. So with Hera in the lead, Poseidon and Athena staged a revolt to remove Zeus from power. They waited until the mighty god was asleep and then bound him tightly and took his thunderbolts.

Restrained and weaponless, Zeus was at their mercy. But the three deities had not decided what to do *after* they captured Zeus. They began to argue, and during their fight, Themis, the goddess of divine justice, snuck over to Zeus, freed him, and returned his weapons.

Zeus's wrath against the deities was great, especially against Hera for her betrayal. To make an example of her, he hung her in the sky with two heavy anvils chained to her feet. Hera was in agony during her punishment. Zeus finally freed her because her moans of pain kept him awake at night!

LOOK OUT, GIRLFRIENDS

Hera punishes anyone who catches Zeus's wandering eye.

Zeus

Even though she was the goddess of marriage, Hera was unable to keep her husband faithful. Hera was a jealous and vengeful goddess. When she couldn't control Zeus's romantic entanglements, Hera took out her anger on his girlfriends and their children.

When Zeus and the mortal princess Semele were awaiting the arrival of their baby Dionysus, Hera disguised herself as Semele's trusted babysitter. In this role, Hera placed doubt in Semele's mind about Zeus's true identity. So Semele asked Zeus to show himself in all his godly splendor. This was more than a mortal could bear, and Zeus's radiance scorched Semele to death.

Io, one of Hera's priestesses, also caught Zeus's eye. To protect her from Hera's jealous rage, Zeus transformed Io into a cow. But Hera hired a giant to hold Io hostage, and later sent a biting fly to torment her.

Hera had a special punishment for Leto. When Leto was expecting Zeus's twins, Apollo and Artemis, Hera would not allow her to give birth on solid ground or anywhere that the sun shone. Finally with the help of several deities, Leto found a safe island, Delos, to have her twins.

What's going on back there?

Io

Hera

She ZAPPED him!

HERA HATES HERACLES

Hera makes Heracles' life horrible!

The great hero Heracles, a son of Zeus and Alcmene, inspired more wrath from Hera than perhaps any of Zeus's other children. (Interestingly, the name Heracles literally translates to "glory of Hera.")

Even before Heracles was born, Hera was cooking up ways to cause trouble for him. For example, Heracles was next in line to inherit the rule of the city of Argos. But Hera prevented Heracles from being born when he was supposed to be. Instead, a baby boy named Eurystheus was born first—and he, rather than Heracles, became ruler of Argos.

Then, when Heracles was just a tiny baby, Hera tried to kill him by sending two poisonous snakes to his crib! But the infant already showed signs of the strength that would make him a legend. He strangled the two snakes and killed them with his bare hands.

When he was an adult, Heracles married a woman named Megara and started a family with her.

But Hera wasn't finished tormenting Heracles yet. She cursed him with madness, causing him to murder his whole family, including Megara! As punishment for his crimes, Heracles had to undertake twelve grueling labors. But even after he successfully completed each task, Heracles' life was complicated—to say the least. His next wife, Deianeira, accidentally poisoned him with a shirt soaked in toxic blood from the monster Hydra. In agonizing pain, Heracles begged to be put out of his misery.

When he died, the gods rewarded all the heroic acts in his life by taking him to Olympus, where Heracles became an **immortal** god. As for Hera, she finally forgave Heracles when he became her son-in-law by marrying her daughter Hebe.

"I hate Heracles. I really, really, really hate him."

What have I ever done to you?

Heracles

Telephus

"I love all my children just the same—really!

MOMMY DEAREST

Hera plays favorites and Hephaestus gets the boot.

Hera and Zeus were the proud parents of some godly offspring: Ares, the god of war; Hebe, the goddess of youth; and Eileithyia, the goddess of childbirth. But Hera's son Hephaestus, god of fire and blacksmithing, got nothing but loathing from his mother. Why? Because Hephaestus was just plain ugly!

When Hephaestus was born, Hera was so disgusted by him that she literally threw him off Mount Olympus, crippling the poor little baby. When Hephaestus grew up into a talented and accomplished god, Hera regretted having treated him so badly. She urged him to return to Mount Olympus, which he did, but only to get revenge.

The crafty god made a magical golden throne for Hera that bound her tightly and wouldn't release her! Eventually, the god Dionysus tricked Hephaestus into releasing

Help, let me off.

Hera

Hera, and mother and son reconciled. According to some stories, Hephaestus even took Hera's side against Zeus during an argument.

REALITY CHECK

An echo is a sound you hear that has been reflected (bounced back) from a hard surface. Although all sound waves can be reflected, only reflected sounds you can hear distinctly are called echoes.

ECHO'S CURSE … CURSE … CURSE …

A nymph covers for a god, betrays a goddess, and runs out of things to say.

Echo was a lovely mountain **nymph** and one of Hera's servants. Because of her position—and her closeness to Hera—Zeus devised a cunning plan for Echo. He used the chatty nymph to distract Hera when he wanted to strike up a new romance. So whenever Zeus started wooing another conquest, Echo would find Hera and start talking nonstop to distract her.

When Hera found out what Echo was doing, she punished her severely: From then on, Echo could only repeat the words of others. And that's why in some places your voice will echo!

79

ANTIOPE

Satyr, yeah, right ... that princess had to know it was my guy.

DIE!

Sent a fly to bite her!

IO

ALCMENE

Sent baby Heracles a special gift from Snakes-R-Us.

Heracles

LEDA

Made a pillow for her. And guess whose feathers I stuffed it with!

EX-WIVES

METIS   THEMIS   EURYNOME

The ex-wives' club. Zeus left you in the dust, girls!

Sounds Like: hes'-tee-uh

Roman Name: Vesta

Generation:
- ☐ Titan
- ☑ Olympian
- ☐ Other

Divine Powers: Family life
The hearth

Attributes: Family meal
Flowering branch
Kettle
Sacred fire
Veil

Who wants s'more?

Top 10 Things to Know About Me:

10. I refused to marry Poseidon or Apollo; I want to remain a maiden forever.

9. I'm an important goddess because, back in the day, the hearth was the center of family life.

8. I was one of the original twelve Olympians. I gave up my spot to Dionysus, or maybe it was Aphrodite.

7. I never take sides in wars or arguments.

6. I'm the eldest sibling of Hera, Demeter, Zeus, Hades, and Poseidon.

5. I invented houses and how to build them.

4. Every city in ancient Greece had a sacred hearth dedicated to me, with a flame that never went out.

3. The first part of every sacrifice was offered to me.

2. I'm the kindest and most gentle goddess of all.

1. I tend the hearth on Mount Olympus. Nobody roasts marshmallows like I do!

Family, Flings, Friends, and Foes

▼ Parents

Cronus and Rhea

▼ Siblings

Zeus

Hades

Poseidon

Hera

Demeter

▼ Friends

Dionysus

Aphrodite

HESTIA

PLAYING WITH FIRE

Come sit by the fire! Would you like a piece of fresh-baked bread?—*Ow*! That fresh-baked bread is *hot*! How about some tasty stew? Anyway, I just love tending the fire. It's so cozy and safe here—not like fighting in a horrible war or dealing with the attentions of a love-struck god. I'll just add more wood to the fire. Uh-oh, those flames are leaping *awfully* high. What's the roof made of ? Straw? Well in that case—*run*!

HESTIA

"Come sit by my fire!"

MYTHLOPEDIA

Εστια

IT'S GREEK TO ME

Hestia ruled over public hearths in cities, as well as hearths in homes. Each time a new colony was established in ancient Greece, its public hearth would be kindled with a flame from Hestia's hearth.

"No more roughing it— thanks to me!"

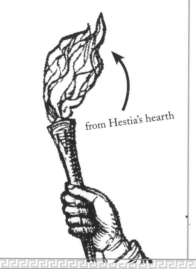

from Hestia's hearth

HOME AND HEARTH

Hestia invents houses and hangs out hearthside.

Hestia was the goddess of the hearth, or fireplace. The hearth located inside each ancient homestead was a source of warmth and light, and a place to cook food. The hearth was perhaps the most important feature of a Greek house—so it is only fitting that Hestia was the keeper of the hearth, since she invented houses and the art of building them! Her invention helped humans create warm, safe, permanent shelters and led them to give up their **nomadic** existence of living in tents or caves. She was, therefore, universally revered by the Greeks. Though there were few temples dedicated to Hestia, each town had a public hearth in her honor that held an eternally lit flame, and she occupied a special place as the guardian of the family hearth in each home.

HOT!

"Why make war when we can relax by the fire instead?"

Yum!

Hestia

PEACE OUT
The goddess of the hearth keeps her cool.

Hestia had a peaceful and gentle nature, unlike the other gods and goddesses of Olympus, who were known for their public squabbles and feuds. She did everything in her power to avoid the conflicts of gods and **mortals** alike.

Hestia was a daughter of the Titans Cronus and Rhea. Her siblings included Poseidon, Hades, Demeter, Hera, and even Zeus himself—**deities** who were involved in many fierce exchanges. But Hestia was content to lead a quiet existence tending the hearth, and she avoided the excitement and drama of wars, feuds, and fights. In fact, some stories claim that Hestia voluntarily abandoned her place on Olympus to tend the hearth fires so that conflict would be avoided when

Dionysus (or perhaps Aphrodite) joined the Olympians, since 12—not 13—was a pattern number to the ancient Greeks.

DOMESTIC DIVA MAKES GOOD

Hearth Goddess's Line of Home Goods Available Now

MOUNT OLYMPUS— Since the debut of *Hearthside With Hestia*, a monthly magazine of home-making tips, this shy and peaceful goddess has exploded onto the scene as one to watch. What's next for the domestic diva? Two cookbooks, *Hearth Cookin'* and *Homestyle Fireside Favorites*, followed by Hestia-branded fireplace tools and kitchenware, including kettles and spoons. Homemakers everywhere agree: Since Hestia started sharing her expertise, hearth-keeping's never been easier!

BAN ON BOYS
Hestia vows to be single forever.

Like Artemis and Athena, Hestia was fiercely protective of her maidenhood. After Zeus overthrew Cronus, both Apollo and Poseidon sought her hand in marriage—but Hestia wanted no part of a romantic relationship with either one! She vowed by Zeus's head to remain **chaste**, rejecting both gods' proposals and helping keep the peace on Olympus by not favoring one god over another. Zeus rewarded Hestia's behavior with a great honor: The first part of every sacrifice was dedicated to her.

REALITY CHECK
In the ancient Greek practice of sacrifice, a tame animal was killed and part of it was offered to the gods. Animals were sacrificed in order to repay the gods for something they had done or in hopes of receiving their favor.

Want to know more? Go to:
http://www.historyforkids.org/learn/greeks/religion/sacrifice.htm

▼ Profile of Iris

Sounds Like:	**eye'-ris**
Roman Name:	**Iris**
Aliases:	**Arcus**
Generation:	☐ **Titan**
	☑ **Olympian**
	✓ **Other**

Divine Powers:	**Messenger to the gods**
	Rainbow

Attributes:	**Golden pitcher**
	Golden wings
	Staff

Top 10 Things to Know About Me:

10. I use a rainbow as a bridge between the heavens and Earth.

9. Zephyrus, the god of the warm west wind, was my boyfriend.

8. Zephyrus and I have a son named Pothos.

7. Zeus sends me to get water from the River Styx whenever the Olympians need to swear an oath (or when he needs to find out if someone is lying).

6. My sisters, the Harpies, were going to die for tormenting Phineus—but I saved them.

5. I'm Hera's special messenger.

4. My pal Hermes is also a messenger of the gods.

3. When I deliver messages to mortals, I assume the form of someone they know.

2. Sometimes I'm the personification of the rainbow.

1. I move water between clouds and the earth, helping new rainbows form.

▼ Family, Flings, Friends, and Foes

▼ Parents	▼ Siblings	▼ Offspring	▼ Flings	▼ Friends			▼ Foes
Thaumas and Electra	The Harpies	Pothos	Zephyrus	Hera	Hermes	Leto	Demeter

IRIS
SPILL IT!

Well, well, well. It seems *someone* hasn't been honest with Zeus. You want to do this the easy way or the hard way? Easy way: 'Fess up and take your punishment like a god. Hard way: Why don't you swear an oath on this water from the River Styx? Take a sip. If you're telling the truth, you have *nothing* to worry about. It's only the liars who will fall into a coma and be exiled from Olympus for nine long years!

Bottoms up!

How does she always know when I'm lying?

Pinocchio

IRIS

"She's a rainbow."

MYTHLOPEDIA

IT'S GREEK TO ME

Iris is an example of a goddess who's the **personification** of a natural phenomenon—in this case, a rainbow. Iris could turn into a rainbow and form an arc between Olympus and Earth when she needed to deliver a message. When ancient Greeks saw a rainbow, they knew that Iris was at work!

RAINBOW RIDE

Iris takes a ride down a rainbow to deliver very important messages.

Iris, like the Olympian god Hermes, had a very important job: She was a messenger of the gods, especially for the almighty Zeus and the goddess Hera. In this role, she delivered news and correspondence from Olympus to Earth by traveling on a bridge made from a rainbow. Iris was also a personification of the rainbow. According to some stories, Iris became a rainbow when she needed to travel. When a rainbow arched across the sky, it was really Iris on her way to deliver a message! Hera especially made use of Iris's services, and the two goddesses became close.

"Wheeeeeeeee!"

Hera

A SIP OF STYX

Iris carries water from the River Styx.

The dreaded River Styx served as a border between the land of the living and the **Underworld,** the realm of dead souls. Each dead soul had to cross the River Styx in order to reach the Underworld. But the Styx had two other important purposes. When a god swore an oath by the River Styx, the oath took on greater power. A **deity** who broke the oath would suffer awful consequences. And a sip of water from the Styx would reveal if someone was telling the truth or lying.

Fetching water from the River Styx was a special task for Iris, since most of the other deities (except for Hermes, another messenger god) avoided the Underworld entirely. Zeus trusted Iris alone with this important duty, and used the water she brought from the Styx to settle many disputes.

Truth serum!

STYX WATER

HARPIES' HEROINE

Iris protects her stinky sisters to the end.

It may come as a surprise to learn that the beautiful goddess of the rainbow was a sister of the hideous Harpies— monstrous creatures with the heads of women and the bodies of vultures. These horrible beasts were also known as demons of death, and they often harassed **mortals**.

The blind **seer** Phineus was one of their targets for punishment after he slipped up and told some of the gods' secrets to mortals. The Harpies tormented him by stealing or contaminating his food. Two Argonauts (crew members on the ship the *Argo*) planned to slay the Harpies to put an end to their torture of Phineus—until Iris stepped in. She promised that if the Argonauts spared the Harpies, her stinky sisters would no longer bother Phineus. The Harpies were lucky to have a sister as devoted as Iris!

REALITY CHECK

A monkey being preyed on by a harpy eagle might feel tormented, just like Phineus! Harpy eagles can swoop down and snatch up monkeys as heavy as 17 pounds.

Want to know more? Go to:
http://www.sandiegozoo.org/animalbytes/
t-harpy_eagle.html

They got the mean gene!

The Harpies

Harpy Eagle

"They're not hideous, they're my sisters!"

Profile of Leto

Sounds Like: lee'-toh

Roman Name: Latona

Generation: ✓ Titan
☐ Olympian
☐ Other

Divine Powers: Motherhood

Attributes: Island of Delos
Veil

Top 10 Things to Know About Me:

10. I may be a Titan, but Apollo and Artemis call me Mom.

9. Hera hates me because her hubby, Zeus, was my twins' daddy.

8. Hera wouldn't allow me to give birth on land or anywhere the sun shone.

7. Poseidon found the perfect place for me to have my babies—a floating island called Delos.

6. Goddesses bribed Iris to bring Eileithyia, goddess of childbirth, to help me deliver my twins at last.

5. My parents are the Titans Coeus and Phoebe.

4. The monster Python tried to kill me because it was prophesied that my son would kill him.

3. Tityus tried to attack me—but my twins or maybe Zeus killed him!

2. I turned some Lycians into frogs because they wouldn't let me drink from their lake. I'm still laughing about that one!

1. Niobe made a BIG mistake when she bragged that just because she had more kids she was a better mother than me!

Special delivery!

Family, Flings, Friends, and Foes

▼ Parents	▼ Siblings	▼ Offspring		▼ Flings	▼ Friends		

Coeus and Phoebe	Asteria	Apollo	Artemis	Zeus	Poseidon	Eileithyia	Iris

LETO
TWIN TROUBLES

Brrrring! Hi, my name is Leto. I'm a friend of Zeus and I'm looking for a place to have my babies. Hello? *Hello*? Rats, they hung up. *Brrrring*! Hi, is this the island of Rhodes? Can you tell me if you have any shady spots where I can have my twins? ... Hello? Are you there? Oh, no! Another hang-up. Hera is torturing me! There's one more. *Brrrring*! Is this Delos? I need a safe spot where I can have my babies. You do? Hooray!

Puh-lease!

▼ Foes

Hera	Niobe	Python	Tityus	Lycians

stork

LETO

"Mom's the word!"

MYTHLOPEDIA

Λητω

"Note to self: Next time, don't fall for Hera's husband!"

DIVINE MOTHER

Leto delivers twins on a quiet little island.

Leto was a beautiful goddess who caught the eye of the mighty god Zeus. When Zeus's wife, Hera, discovered that Leto was pregnant with Zeus's twins, she was outraged. To punish Leto, Hera declared that she could not give birth on solid ground, or anywhere that the sun shone.

Poor Leto was desperate to deliver her twins—but couldn't find a place to have them. Everywhere she went she was turned away. Finally Poseidon, the god of the sea, took pity on Leto and guided her to the floating island of Delos. The little island met Hera's conditions once Poseidon covered it with waves so that the sun wouldn't shine on it.

But Hera wasn't done tormenting Leto yet. Next she prevented Eileithyia, her daughter and the goddess of childbirth, from helping Leto with the birth. But other goddesses bribed Iris to bring Eileithyia, and Leto finally had her twins. First Leto gave birth to Artemis, who then helped her mother deliver Apollo. Leto showed her appreciation to the island of Delos by granting it four sturdy columns to keep it anchored so that it would no longer float.

Delos

NASTY NIOBE
Niobe learns not to challenge a goddess.

Much of Leto's **renown** came from her famous children: Apollo and Artemis were powerful Olympian **deities** indeed. But a **mortal** woman named Niobe learned a terrible lesson—and paid a dreadful price—when she underestimated Leto's importance.

Niobe, who was the mother of fourteen children (seven sons and seven daughters), bragged that since she had seven times as many children as Leto, she was more important than the goddess.

Apollo and Artemis were not about to let anybody insult their mother—especially a mere mortal. With their sharp arrows and accurate aim, Apollo and Artemis killed each and every one of Niobe's children—Apollo, the boys, and Artemis, the girls.

Overwhelmed by grief and shame, Niobe couldn't stop weeping. To stop her pitiful cries, Zeus finally turned her into a rock. To this day, after it rains the rock appears to weep—silently, though.

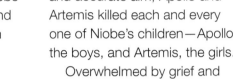

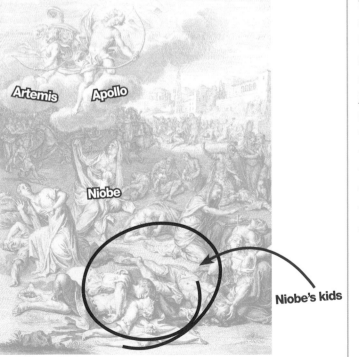

Artemis **Apollo**

Niobe

Niobe's kids

Who knew she was a goddess?

LOOK OUT, LYCIANS!
Petty peasants pay the price for their rudeness.

After giving birth to Apollo and Artemis, Leto wrapped up her babies and traveled to Lycia. Along the way, she grew thirsty and exhausted. When she came to a pond of cool, clear water in Lycia, Leto dropped to her knees and prepared to drink from it. But a crowd of rude Lycians stopped her and refused to let the weary goddess drink from their pond. Ignorant of her true status, they jeered at her and taunted her. Leto begged for a little water to drink, but they denied her. Then the Lycians jumped into the pond and stamped in the mud so that the water grew cloudy and dirty, unfit to drink. Enough was enough for Leto. The enraged goddess transformed the Lycians into frogs, cursing them to a lifetime spent croaking in the mud!

"I hope you all croak!"

▼ Profile of The Muses

Roman Name: the Camenae

Greek Name: the Mousai

Generation:
- ☐ Titan
- ☐ Olympian
- ☑ Other

Divine Powers: Artistic, intellectual, and scientific pursuits

That was brilliant!

Top 10 Things to Know About Us:

10. At first there were just three of us, but we expanded to nine to cover more arts and sciences.

9. Apollo is our leader.

8. Zeus, ruler of the gods, is our father.

7. Mnemosyne, the Titan goddess of memory, is our mother—a good thing since we have a lot of memorizing to do!

6. We dance and sing at festivals held to honor gods and heroes.

5. Writers often call on us for inspiration. When we hear the plea "O Muse," we get busy.

4. We punish anyone who claims to be more talented than we are.

3. Most of us have children, and some of us have been involved with some VIGs (Very Important Gods): Apollo, Hermes, and even Zeus!

2. Olympus, Helicon, and Parnassus are areas that are very important to us.

1. We share similar interests with our friends the Graces.

He's a god.

▼ Family, Flings, Friends, and Foes

▼ Parents

Zeus and Mnemosyne

▼ Offspring

Orpheus

Hyacinthus

The Sirens

The Corybantes

Linus

▼ Flings

Apollo

Ares

Arcas

The MUSES

OLYMPIAN IDOL

Give it up for Apollo—nice lyre solo, Bro.
Judges? Let's start with you, Euterpe.
"Listen up, dawg. A little pitchy but
overall, it was da bomb."
Terpsichore? "Apollo, you touched my
soul and showed who you really are. A
god! I'm so proud of you." Polyhymnia?
"A-b-s-o-l-u-t-e-l-y brilliant, Apollo.
Of course, I picked the song."
The Muses have spoken.
Now it's up to the audience.
Who will be the *next* Olympian
Idol, Marsyas or Apollo?

REALITY CHECK

Over time, translations of Homer's *Odyssey* have differed, but each of them has started by asking for the Muses' help in telling the story.

Homer

Thank you. Thank you very much.

Apollo

▼ Friends

Achelous

Hermes

Zeus

The Graces

Dionysus

Apollo

The MUSES

"We're inspired."

MYTHOPEDIA

Μουσαι

IT'S GREEK TO ME

Each of the nine Muses has a specialty:

➤ **CALLIOPE**, the Muse of **epic** and heroic poetry, holds a writing tablet and **stylus**.

➤ **CLIO**, the Muse of history, holds a roll of parchment.

➤ **ERATO**, the Muse of lyric and love poetry, plays a lyre.

➤ **EUTERPE**, the Muse of music, especially wind instruments, plays a double flute.

➤ **MELPOMENE**, the Muse of tragic poetry, holds a tragic mask.

➤ **POLYHYMNIA**, the Muse of sacred poetry and hymns, holds her fingers to her lips.

➤ **TERPSICHORE**, the Muse of dance, choral poetry, and song, holds a lyre.

➤ **THALIA**, the Muse of comic poetry and poetry about rural life, holds a comic mask and a shepherd's crook.

➤ **URANIA**, the Muse of astronomy, sits beside a globe and holds compasses for tracking the stars.

MEET THE MUSES

Nine goddesses with great talents. Which one should you call on for inspiration?

The Muses were nine tremendously talented goddesses, each one corresponding to an artistic or intellectual pursuit. They were the daughters of Zeus and the Titan Mnemosyne, the goddess of memory—an appropriate parentage, since the gift of memory is an advantage for someone aspiring to greatness in any field!

In the earliest stories, the Muses were three nameless goddesses who spoke the chorus of epic poems or plays. Later, their number grew to nine, and each one specialized in a particular field. Each Muse's **attributes** represented her specialty. With such a vast array of talents, the Muses entertained the **deities** at banquets and festivals. They also have been called on by **mortals** seeking inspiration.

Apollo

The Muses

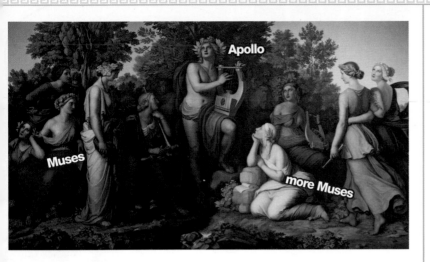

Apollo

Muses

more Muses

PAGING MR. MUSAGETES!

Mr. Musagetes leads his talented Muses.

As god of the arts, Apollo was the leader of the Muses. In fact, one of his nicknames was Apollo Musagetes (the translation of *Musagetes* is "leader of the Muses"). Apollo helped the Muses prepare for the banquets and festivals at which they entertained deities. Their performances were a way to honor gods or goddesses. Often, the Muses performed in a chorus that was directed by Apollo.

Apollo led the Muses and they were only too happy to follow, since they all loved the charming god. Some of the Muses even became mothers of his children—Calliope and Apollo were the parents of Orpheus, a famous musician, and Terpsichore and Apollo were the parents of Linus, a famous poet.

REALITY CHECK

Among the great performers whose careers have been launched at the historic Apollo Theater in New York City are Ella Fitzgerald, Billie Holiday, Stevie Wonder, and Michael Jackson.

Want to know more? Go to:www.apollotheatre.org

"Apollo really appreciates the arts—and us!"

ONE NIGHT ONLY!
LIVE AT THE APOLLO THEATER
THE MUSES

JUDGMENT DAY

Marsyas loses a battle of the bands—and his skin.

The **satyr** Marsyas challenged Apollo to a musical contest. He would play the flute and Apollo, the lyre. The winner could do what he wished with the loser. The Muses served as the contest judges—because who could better determine which contestant was more talented? No one was surprised that Apollo, with his brilliant musical skills, won easily. And what about the loser? The unfortunate Marsyas was hung from a tree and skinned alive!

O MUSE ...

The Muses inspire great works of art and scholarship.

Because of their powerful artistic gifts, it was hoped that the favor of a Muse would bring great inspiration to a mere mortal. In the opening lines of numerous poems and plays, writers often ask for inspiration or aid from a Muse. This tradition lasted beyond the age of famed Greek and Roman poets such as Homer and Virgil. More than a thousand years later, William Shakespeare opened some of his plays and sonnets with a plea for inspiration from a Muse!

99

▼ Profile of Persephone

Sounds Like: pur-sef'-uh-nee

Roman Name: Proserpina

Aliases: Kore, Despoena

Generation:
- ☐ Titan
- ☐ Olympian
- ☑ Other

Divine Powers: Queen of the Underworld

Attributes: Grain
Pomegranate
Torch

> The Underworld is such a downer.

Top 10 Things to Know About Me:

10. My parents are Zeus, ruler of the gods, and Demeter, goddess of the grain harvest.

9. My dad promised my gloomy uncle Hades that I'd go with him to the Underworld.

8. Hades swept me off my feet, literally!

7. While my mother searched the world for me, crops died and people starved.

6. Just because I ate some pomegranate seeds I'm stuck in the Underworld for part of every year. What a raw deal!

5. When I'm in the Underworld winter comes, and nothing grows until I return to Earth in the spring.

4. I trampled Minthe because Hades loved her—and the mint plant sprang up from the ground.

3. Orpheus broke our hearts with his beautiful music. Even the rulers of the Underworld have feelings.

2. I loved Adonis and tried to keep him from Aphrodite.

1. I'm the queen of the dead. Talk about boring!

▼ Family, Flings, Friends, and Foes

▼ Parents	▼ Siblings				▼ Spouse	▼ Flings
Zeus and Demeter	Apollo	Artemis	Ares	Arion	Hades	Hermes

PERSEPHONE

QUEEN OF THE *WHAT?*

Whoa. One minute I'm picking flowers with my BFFs, the next minute Uncle Hades is dragging me underground! This placc is way creepy. Likc, is cverybody here *dead*, or what? Don't answer that. I never thought being a queen would be so depressing. And I miss my mom. She's gonna get me out of here, right? I guess I'll just snack on these pomegranate seeds while I wait … and wait … and wait …

You'll feel better after you've eaten, I promise!

Hades

REALITY CHECK

The pomegranate, a fruit associated with Persephone, is a sacred symbol in many of the world's religions. Because it is thought to have medicinal properties, it is also a symbol for many medical associations.

Want to know more? Go to: http://www.pomegranates.org/

▼ Friends

 Adonis

 Artemis

 Athena

 Nymphs

 Orpheus

 Tiresias

▼ Foes

 Minthe

 Leuce

 Aphrodite

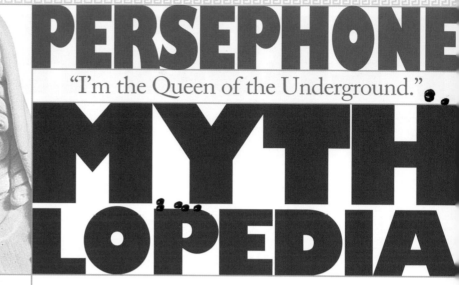

PERSEPHONE

"I'm the Queen of the Underground."

MYTH LOPEDIA

Περσεφονη

IT'S GREEK TO ME

Together, Hades and Persephone ruled over the **Underworld**. The regions of the Underworld, or death realm, included Tartarus, Asphodel Meadows, and the Elysian Field. The souls of the dead were transported across the River Styx by the ferryman Charon, and escorted into the gates, where they were prevented from leaving by Cerberus, Hades' guard dog.

DO NOT ENTER!

The Necromanteion of Ephyra in Thrace

KIDNAPPED!

Hades takes a liking to his niece—then takes her for his queen.

Persephone was the daughter of the mighty god Zeus and Demeter, the goddess of the harvest. Her uncle Hades, ruler of the Underworld, wanted Persephone for his queen. With Zeus's approval, Hades roared to Earth in his **chariot** and kidnapped Persephone. Demeter heard her daughter's cries for help, but could not find her anywhere.

When she learned what Hades had done, Demeter refused to attend to her duties until he returned her daughter. This resulted in a terrible **famine** on Earth. People suffered so much that Zeus finally insisted Hades return Persephone to Demeter—but only if she had not eaten or drunk anything in the Underworld. Unfortunately, she had snacked on a few pomegranate seeds that Hades had given to her, so a compromise was reached: Persephone would spend part of each year living in the Underworld, and part of the year with her mother on Earth.

This myth explains the change of seasons: When Persephone is in the Underworld, Demeter grieves and abandons her duties caring for the crops, leading to the barren seasons of autumn and winter. When Persephone is returned to her mother, Demeter rejoices, and fruits, vegetables, and flowers grow once more during spring and summer.

From: maiden@godmail.com
To: GrainGoddess@godmail.com
Subject: GET ME OUT OF HERE!

Mom! I hate it here soooo much! Hades won't let me leave. This place is full of dead people! And it's getting really crowded down here—what is going on up there? I miss you tons. SAVE ME!
xoxo,
Persephone

From: GrainGoddess@godmail.com
To: maiden@godmail.com
Subject: Re: GET ME OUT OF HERE!

Honey, I know. I'm working on it. Don't worry about the dead people. There's a little famine going on up here. I've called on your dad to help me get you back. Hang in there.
Love you so much,
Mom
P.S. DON'T EAT ANYTHING!!!

EVIL QUEEN
Persephone isn't shy about showing her harsh side.

Persephone was just a sweet young girl when she became queen of the Underworld. Over time her duties there hardened her heart, since part of her role was to forbid the dead from leaving. She earned the nickname "Iron Queen" because she was so rigid. Persephone's dark side showed in other ways, as well. When her husband, Hades, became romantically involved with a **nymph** named Minthe, Persephone grew so jealous that she trampled Minthe into the ground. From Minthe's remains sprang the mint plant.

Persephone did have a softer side. The great musician Orpheus journeyed to the Underworld hoping to retrieve his beloved wife, Eurydice, who had died. He played the lyre so beautifully that Persephone allowed Eurydice to leave the Underworld—as long as Orpheus didn't look at her on the way out. Orpheus hurried through the Underworld, with Eurydice following behind him. They had almost reached he world of the living when Orpheus glanced over his shoulder to make sure Eurydice was behind him. Suddenly Eurydice vanished into the Underworld for good.

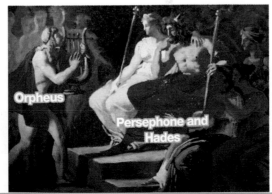

Orpheus

Persephone and Hades

"Hands off my boyfriend, Aphrodite!"

ALL ADONIS, ALL THE TIME
Persephone and Aphrodite share the most handsome man of all time.

After the beautiful youth Adonis was orphaned, the goddess of love, Aphrodite, delivered him to Persephone in a locked chest for safekeeping. Aphrodite knew that Adonis's exquisite beauty would attract the attention of the other gods and goddesses, and she wanted to keep him for herself. Aphrodite's instinct was correct. The minute Persephone saw Adonis, she fell in love with him, too—and refused to return him to Aphrodite! Their argument over Adonis was so fierce that Zeus finally intervened, declaring that Adonis should spend four months of the year with Aphrodite, four months with Persephone, and have the remaining four months to himself. Adonis, though, had fallen in love with Aphrodite, so he chose to spend his portion of the year with her as well.

Profile of Rhea

Sounds Like: ree'-uh

Roman Name: Ops

Aliases: Magna Mater
Cybele, Mater Turrita

Generation: ☑ Titan
☐ Olympian
☐ Other

Divine Powers: Fertility

Attributes: Chariot pulled by lions
Crown with towers on it
Cymbals
Lion
Scepter

Top 10 Things to Know About Me:

10. My dad, Uranus, locked me in Tartarus with the rest of my brothers and sisters.

9. I married my brother Cronus—don't ask!

8. Cronus and I produced the first generation of Olympians.

7. Cronus swallowed our kids to prevent them from overthrowing him—but I hid Zeus away.

6. Our mom, Gaea, helped me find a way to trick Cronus.

5. My son Zeus freed his siblings from Cronus and took over the world.

4. I am known as the Great Mother—and that's what one of my names means.

3. Though my children are the Olympians, I don't live on Mount Olympus with them.

2. I guard towns.

1. Fierce animals don't frighten me. *Roar*!

Rock wrapped in blanket to look like a baby

Family, Flings, Friends, and Foes

▼ Parents	▼ Siblings	▼ Spouse	▼ Offspring					
Uranus and Gaea	The Titans	Cronus	Zeus	Hades	Poseidon	Hera	Demeter	Hestia

RHEA
MOTHER KNOWS BEST

Cronus, I know that becoming a dad is stressful. It's a big responsibility to have a little god or goddess depend on you for everything! There's so much to teach them—how to transform, how to use their powers, and how to curse mortals. I bet that most new dads worry a lot when they learn there's a little deity on the way. But swallowing your children is no way to deal with your fears! Won't you please leave this one alone? *Please?*

REALITY CHECK

Thank you, Mom! The tradition of honoring mothers may have begun in ancient Greece. There, a celebration was held each spring to honor the mother of the gods and goddesses. In the United States, Mother's Day, the second Sunday of May each year, became a national holiday in 1914.

Want to know more? Go to: http://www.holidays.net/mother/

▼ Flings

Iasion

▼ Friends

Pelops

The Kouretes

Pan

▼ Foes

Cronus

Uranus

Pyrrhos

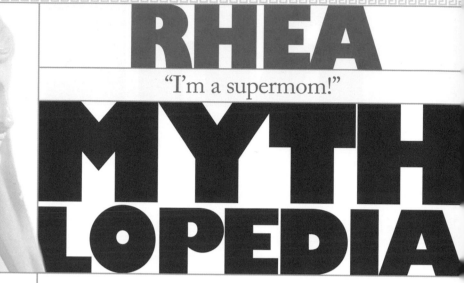

RHEA

"I'm a supermom!"

MYTH LOPEDIA

Ρεα

IT'S GREEK TO ME

Zeus and the Olympians are the most famous Greek gods—but did you know that there was a generation of gods that came before them? First came Uranus (sky) and Gaea (earth), whose children were the powerful gods known as the Titans. Eventually, the Titan Cronus overthrew Uranus, and then Cronus became the ruling god. Later, Cronus's own children (Zeus and the other Olympians) overthrew him and the other Titans, and Zeus became the ultimate ruler.

A DUD OF A DAD

Rhea gets locked up in Tartarus with her siblings.

Rhea and her siblings were Titans, the generation of **deities** that came before the Olympians. Her parents were Uranus, the sky, and Gaea, the earth. Uranus and Gaea had many powerful children, and Uranus feared that they would one day overthrow him and force him out of power. To safeguard his rule, he locked all his kids, including Rhea, in Tartarus, deep inside the earth. This was very painful for Gaea (the earth itself), who wanted her children to be free. So Gaea convinced her sons to attack Uranus. The youngest, Cronus, slashed Uranus with a sickle. Wounded, Uranus limped away, and the Titans were freed!

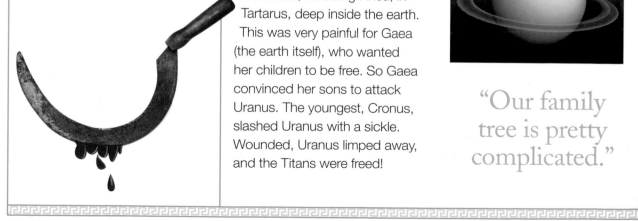

REALITY CHECK

Is there a planet Herschel? No, but there almost was. Uranus, the seventh planet in the solar system, was discovered in 1781 by British astronomer William Herschel. Some people wanted to name the new planet after Herschel. Fortunately, astronomers named it Uranus, for the Greek god of the heavens.

Want to know more? Go to:
http://www.nineplanets.org/uranus.html

"Our family tree is pretty complicated."

BROTHERLY LOVE

Rhea watches as Cronus takes after her old man.

After Cronus attacked Uranus, he became the ruler of the Titans. Then he and Rhea started a family. But when Uranus and Gaea prophesied that one of Cronus's children would overthrow him, Cronus started to fear his own kids—just as his father had before him. So Cronus took drastic measures. As each of his children was born, Cronus swallowed the baby whole! One by one, Hestia, Hera, Demeter, Poseidon, and Hades were gulped down by their dad, just moments after their birth.

Rhea soon grew tired of Cronus's barbaric behavior; she wanted her babies! Rhea turned to her mother, Gaea, who helped her devise a plan. When her next child, Zeus, was born, Rhea hid him away in a cave. She then presented Cronus with a stone wrapped in a baby blanket. Cronus didn't look at the stone; he just popped it in his mouth and swallowed it as he had his other children. Zeus was safe!

Zeus later helped free his siblings, then waged a war against Cronus, called the Titanomachy. Zeus and the other Olympians won the war, and the Titans who had opposed him were once again imprisoned in Tartarus for their defiance. This ushered in the age of Olympian rule.

TITAN LADIES

Rhea and her sisters are some tough Titans.

Rhea had five sisters: Phoebe, Theia, Tethys, Mnemosyne, and Themis. Each one had a special role. And each was the mother of some very special children. Phoebe was the grandmother of Apollo and Artemis. Theia was the mother of Helios, Eos, and Selene. Mnemosyne, the goddess of memory, was the mother of the nine Muses. Tethys, a **personification** of water, was the wife of Oceanus; their offspring included over six thousand river gods and **nymphs**. Finally, Themis was the guardian of divine law and order. With Zeus, her offspring included the Fates and Dike, goddess of mortal justice.

REALITY CHECK

Titanium, Earth's ninth most abundant element, was named in 1795 by Martin Heinrich Klaproth after the Titans of mythology. Because titanium is as strong as steel but much lighter, it is suitable for use in aviation and astronautics. Its symbol is Ti.

Want to know more? Go to:
http://periodic.lanl.gov/elements/22.htm

Those Olympians are such copycats! We were the originals!

Themis

Yum! A baby!

Rhea

Rock

Cronus

▼ Profile of Selene

Sounds Like: suh-lee'-nee

Roman Name: Luna

Aliases: Mene, Phoebe

Generation:
- ☐ Titan
- ☐ Olympian
- ☑ Other

Divine Powers: The moon

Attributes:
Bull
Crown topped with moon
Flowing robe
Silver chariot
Torch
Winged horse

Top 10 Things to Know About Me:

10. I drive a silver chariot across the sky each night to take the moon on its journey.

9. Sometimes I ride a winged horse to tow the moon across the sky.

8. My brother Helios is god of the sun. He's hot!

7. My sister Eos is goddess of the dawn. She's an early riser.

6. I loved the mortal Endymion, so I begged Zeus to let him choose his own fate. Endymion wanted eternal youth—and eternal sleep!

5. Endymion and I had fifty daughters. Now that is some serious girl power!

4. I had flings with Zeus and Pan.

3. Pan tricked me by dressing up as a white sheep. I rode on his back—and he attacked me!

2. I'm stylin' in my silver robes.

1. I'm not only the goddess of the moon, I'm also the moon itself.

"Honey? HEY, HONEY! Oh, did I wake you?

▼ Family, Flings, Friends, and Foes

▼ Parents

Hyperion and Theia

▼ Siblings

Helios

Eos

▼ Offspring

Ersa

The Menae

Naxos

Nemea

Pandeia

SELENE

THE NIGHT IS YOUNG

Endymion, you know I love you, but I can't spend one more night sitting on this couch and listening to you snore. Come on, let's take the silver chariot for a spin, check out that hot new nightspot, and party with the stars! Endymion? Are you even listening to me? Okay, that's it! If you want to sleep your life away, *fine*, but I'm going to get out there and live a little. And stop drooling on my cushions!

Zzzzzzzzz ...

Endymion

REALITY CHECK

The study of Earth's moon is called selenology, named after Selene.

Want to know more? Go to:
http://www.grc.nasa.gov/
www.K-12/rocket/moon.
html

▼ Flings

Endymion

Pan

Zeus

▼ Friends

Artemis

Hecate

Nyx

SELENE

"Dancing in the moonlight."

MYTH LOPEDIA

Σεληνη

IT'S GREEK TO ME

Selene wasn't only the goddess of the moon—she was also the personification of the moon. From her silver robes to her silver **chariot** to her moon-topped crown, everything about her suggests moonlight.

"By the light of the silvery moon? Hey, that's me!"

SLEEPING BEAUTY

Selene's beloved Endymion sleeps for eternity.

Selene, the goddess of the moon, had many love affairs (although not nearly as many as her sister Eos). During her nightly task of towing the moon across the sky, Selene spied a handsome shepherd named Endymion. Selene fell so deeply in love with Endymion that she asked Zeus to grant the shepherd any wish he desired. Zeus agreed, and Endymion asked for eternal youth. He also asked to sleep forever! Zeus granted his wishes, and Endymion passed eternity never aging—or waking up! That didn't stop Selene from visiting him each night, as she drove across the sky. Together, Selene and Endymion had 50 daughters.

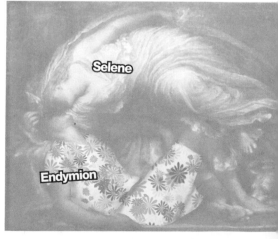

Selene

Endymion

moon_rise: hey guys,
can u help? i m beat ...
want 2 stay in 2nite.
take moon 4 me?
sunshine: no way. 2 tired
from carting sun around
all day
DearDawn: sorry sis. u know
i need my beauty sleep!

MOM IN THE MOON
Selene might just be the Mother of the Year!

As a result of her many romantic involvements, Selene was the mother of a huge brood of children. With Endymion, she had 50 daughters, the Menae, who were goddesses of the lunar months. There were 50 months between each Olympic Games, and each month had a different Mena as its goddess. In addition, Selene had children with Zeus, including Pandeia, goddess of the full moon, Ersa, goddess of the dew, and Nemea, a **nymph**.

REALITY CHECK

Our calendar months vary from 28 to 31 days, but a month based on a lunar calendar follows the cycles of the moon, so its months vary by only a few hours.

Want to know more? Go to:
http://stardate.org/nightsky/moon/

A GOAT-MAN IN SHEEP'S CLOTHING
Pan tricks Selene by dressing up as a sheep!

Half-goat, half-man Pan was famous for falling in love—or lust—with beautiful creatures who had no interest in him. He became infatuated with Selene but she wouldn't pay any attention to him. So Pan came up with a crafty plan to be with her. He wrapped his hairy body in soft, white fleece. Pretending to be a gentle sheep, Pan offered to let Selene ride on his back. The goddess agreed, and when she did, Pan threw off the fleece and attacked her!

REALITY CHECK

The well-known phrase "a wolf in sheep's clothing" is used to describe a person whose actions seem kind but whose motives are actually bad—like Pan!

Want to know more? Go to:
http://www.phrases.org.uk/meanings/wolf-in-sheeps-clothing.html

Baaa ...

innocent bystander

Hee-hee!

Pan

SPOTLIGHT ON NYX
Nyx knows all about the dark side.

Nyx was the **personification** of night and darkness. She was one of the first beings to be born out of **Chaos**, a vast nothingness. Nyx was a frightening figure, with her dark, veiled face and mists of night swirling around her. She was the mother of other personifications, including Light and Day. But she is better known for her dark and disturbing offspring, including Thanatos (god and personification of death), Hypnos (god and personification of sleep), Nemesis (goddess and personification of **retribution**), the Keres (bloodthirsty female spirits), and Eris (goddess and personification of discord). No wonder some people are afraid of the dark!

Nyx

nightlight

FAMILY PORTRAIT

112

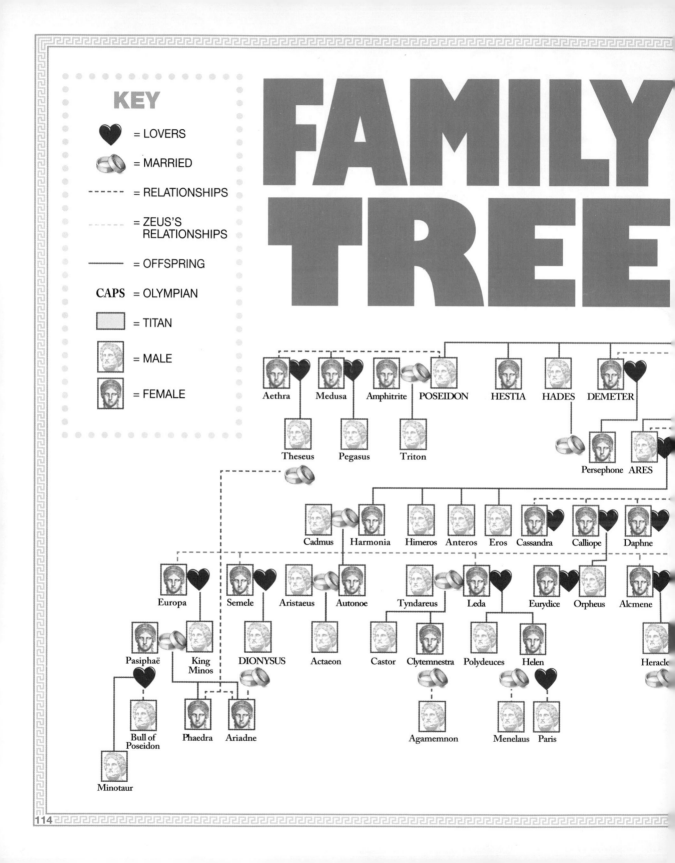

KEY

 = LOVERS

 = MARRIED

------ = RELATIONSHIPS

.... = ZEUS'S RELATIONSHIPS

—— = OFFSPRING

CAPS = OLYMPIAN

▢ = TITAN

▢ = MALE

▢ = FEMALE

FAMILY TREE

Aethra Medusa Amphitrite POSEIDON HESTIA HADES DEMETER

Theseus Pegasus Triton

Persephone ARES

Cadmus Harmonia Himeros Anteros Eros Cassandra Calliope Daphne

Europa Semele Aristaeus Autonoe Tyndareus Leda Eurydice Orpheus Alcmene

Pasiphaë King Minos DIONYSUS Actaeon Castor Clytemnestra Polydeuces Helen Heracle

Bull of Poseidon Phaedra Ariadne Agamemnon Menelaus Paris

Minotaur

114

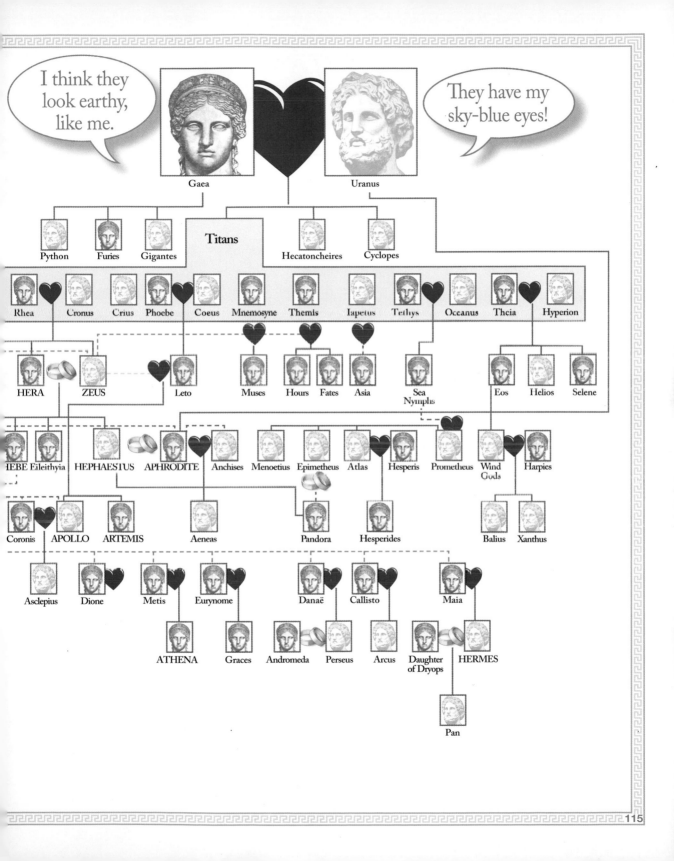

GLOSSARY

acquitted	cleared of wrongdoing
adverse	not favorable; acting in an opposite direction
aegis	a shield covered with goatskin, associated with the god Zeus
afflicted	caused to suffer
ambrosia	the food of the gods
attributes	objects or things closely associated with someone specific
avenged	took revenge for
bedraggled	wet, as if by rain
Chaos	according to Greek mythology, a vast, empty state of nothingness that existed before the earth came into being
chariot	a two-wheeled vehicle drawn by horses
chaste	pure, virginal
chastity	the state of being pure or virginal
cupbearer	one whose job it is to fill wine cups and serve them
deity	a god or goddess

Dryad	a wood nymph
epic	a long poem that tells the story of a hero
famine	an extreme shortage of food that affects people across a wide area
foretell	predict, or tell in advance what will happen
herald	one who delivers messages or announces something to come
immortal	living forever
immortality	the state of living forever
lots	a group of objects (often shards of pottery) used to make a choice by chance
mortal	a human being; also, subject to death
mortality	the state of being subject to death
nectar	the drink of the gods
nomadic	roaming from place to place rather than living in a permanent home

nymphs	female spirits associated with nature
oracle	a priestess or priest who communicated the response of a god to a questioner; also the god's shrine, and the response itself
patronage	the state of being a special guardian or supporter
perjury	swearing to something that is not true
personification	giving human qualities to nonhuman objects or ideas
phenomena	things that can actually be observed, rather than just thought about or imagined
potion	a mixture of liquids given as medicine or for magical reasons
prophecy	a prediction of a future event
prophet	one who foretells the future, often inspired by the gods
renown	fame
retribution	something given in payment, usually as a punishment

satyr	a mythological creature that is part human, part horse or goat
seer	one who sees events that will happen in the future
sow	to plant a crop, especially by scattering seeds
strategy	a careful plan to accomplish a particular goal
transformed	changed in outward appearance
trident	a spear with three prongs
Underworld	in Greek mythology, the world of the dead, ruled by the god Hades

PEGASUS
Zeus placed the winged horse among the stars. Only the front half of his body is shown.

ANDROMEDA
Andromeda was chained to a rock in the sea, threatened by a sea monster, and rescued by the hero Perseus.

CYGNUS
Cygnus the Swan is also known as the Northern Cross. Some mythographers claim the swan is Zeus in disguise.

LYRA
The lyre of the great musician Orpheus was placed among the stars by the Muses.

PERSEUS
The hero slayed the monster Medusa and rescued Andromeda, from Cetus, a sea monster. He is shown holding Medusa's head.

HERACLES
Shown kneeling, holding a club, the great hero Heracles was turned into a constellation by Zeus.

Northern Hemisphere

URSA MAJOR
(Great Bear)
Callisto was turned into a bear and shot by Artemis. Zeus placed her among the stars, where she keeps an eye out for Orion, the hunter.

LEO
(Nemean Lion)
The lion of Nemea was slain by the hero Heracles as one of his twelve labors.

STARS OF GREEK MYTHOLOGY

Many constellations were named for characters in classical mythology. The practice of taking a being or an object and placing it among the stars is called *catasterism*.

ORION
The famed hunter Orion boasted that he would kill every animal on Earth, so Gaea sent a scorpion to sting him. Zeus placed the hunter among the stars and the scorpion nearby *(continues from the Northern Hemisphere to the Southern Hemisphere)*.

CETUS
This sea monster was sent by Poseidon to punish Cassiopeia, the mother of Andromeda, for her vanity.

SCORPIO
Sent by Gaea to sting the hunter Orion, the scorpion is placed near him in the sky to remind him of the consequences of boasting.

CENTAURUS
Centaurus represents the wise Centaur Chiron. Its brightest star, Alpha Centauri, is the closest star to the sun.

ARGO
The ancient constellation Argo Navis, named for the ship that carried Jason and the Argonauts, is made up of three smaller constellations: Puppis (the stern), Carina (the keel), and Vela (the sails).

HYDRA
The serpent was killed by Heracles as another of his twelve labors. In the sky, Hydra is the largest of the 88 constellations *(continues from the Northern Hemisphere to the Southern Hemisphere)*.

Southern Hemisphere

Note: Constellations in this illustration may not be exactly where they appear in the sky. For more accurate charts, go to: www.astronomy.com

119

FURTHER READING

Bolton, Lesley. *The Everything Classical Mythology Book*. Avon, MA: Adams Media, 2002.

Bulfinch, Thomas. *Bulfinch's Greek and Roman Mythology: The Age of Fable.* Mineola, NY: Dover Publications, 2000.

D'Aulaire, Ingri, and Edgar Parin D'Aulaire. *D'Aulaire's Book of Greek Myths.* New York: Random House, Delacorte Press, 1992.

Fleischman, Paul. *Dateline: Troy*. Cambridge, MA: Candlewick Press, 2006.

Hansen, William. *Classical Mythology: A Guide to the Mythical World of the Greeks and Romans*. New York: Oxford University Press, 2005.

Homer. *The Iliad*. Edited by E.V. Rieu. New York: Penguin Classics, 2003.

———. *The Odyssey.* Edited by Bernard Knox. New York: Penguin Classics, 2006.

Osborn, Kevin, and Dana L. Burgess. *The Complete Idiot's Guide to Classical Mythology*. 2nd ed. New York: Penguin, Alpha Books, 2004.

Roberts, Jennifer T., and Tracy Barrett. *The Ancient Greek World*. New York: Oxford University Press, 2004.

Sutcliff, Rosemary. *The Wanderings of Odysseus: The Story of the Odyssey*. New York: Random House, Laurel Leaf, 2005.

———. *Black Ships Before Troy*. London: Frances Lincoln, 2008.

WEB SITES

Encyclopedia Mythica: *http://pantheon.org/*
An online encyclopedia of mythology, folklore, and religion

Greek Mythology: *http://www.greekmythology.com/*
Contains information on gods, goddesses, beasts, and heroes as well as full text of selected books on Greek mythology and literature

Kidipede: Greek Myths: *http://www.historyforkids.org/learn/greeks/religion/greekrelig.htm*
Greek mythology pages of an online encyclopedia of history and science for middle-school students

Mythweb: *http://www.mythweb.com/*
An overview of the Olympians and selected heroes; includes teaching tips

Theoi Greek Mythology: *http://theoi.com/*
Profiles of the Greek gods and goddesses, and other characters from Greek mythology with an emphasis on their appearances in art and literature

INDEX

Marie O'Neill, Creative Director
Cheryl Clark, Editor in Chief
Caroline Anderson, Director of Photography
Cian O'Day; Ed Kasche; Jay Pastorello, Photo Research
SimonSays Design!, Book production and design

Illustrations:
Kevin Brimmer: 75
Paul Meisel: cover, 3, 8–9, 32, 37, 46–47, 51, 63, 64, 112–113, 118–119, 121
G. F. Newland: 80–81
Rupert Van Wyk (Beehive Illustration): 22–23, 98–99, 117
XNR Productions, Inc.: 118–119